Baseball in the 20th Century

Baseball in the 20th Century

Danny Gallagher

Scoop Press
Toronto

Baseball in the 20th Century
Copyright @2000, Danny Gallagher
Printed and bound in Canada

Published by Scoop Press, Toronto
416-535-7738 or 1-888-716-2665

Cover design, typesetting, layout and formatting by
Brian Grebow, BG Communications, Toronto

Front-cover photos: Joe Carter taken by Rick Eglinton, Toronto Star; Reggie Jackson taken by the author; Lee Smith supplied by the Montreal Expos; Babe Ruth supplied by the New York Yankees. Back-cover photos: both Kirby Puckett and Sam Holman taken by the author.
Photo of the author taken by Delight Rogers.

Canadian Cataloguing in Publication data

Gallagher, Danny
Baseball in the 20th Century

Includes index and photos.
ISBN 0-968-1859-3-2

1. Baseball — History. 2. Baseball players — Biography. I. Title

GV862.5G34 2000   796.357'09   C99-933036-5

Contents

Acknowledgments

• Thanks to all those who were so generous with their time in granting me interviews in helping me put this book together. Without anecdotes, a book is next to impossible to write. Special thanks to people like Joe Carter, Kirk Gibson, Bill Mazeroski, Bucky Dent, Rickey Henderson, Dennis Eckersley, Lee Smith and Larry Barnett.

• My thanks go out to all the media organizations and reference-book companies that provided background information: New York Times, New York Daily News, Toronto Star, Toronto Globe and Mail, Toronto Sun, Associated Press, MacMillan's The Baseball Encyclopedia, The Ballplayers, Baseball Legends.

• Thank goodness for the microfilms available for viewing at the Metropolitan Toronto Reference Library, a facility of which residents in the Toronto area should be might proud. Also, thanks to the National Library of Canada.

• Much gratitude is expressed to all the teams and card companies which supplied photographs.

Foreword

There may be arguments where baseball had its birth but evidence seems to indicate that the venue was a spot in St. Mary's, Ontario, southwest of Toronto in the 1800s but it was in the 20th century that the game enjoyed both its growth and decline in popularity.

Growth abound in the 1920s when Babe Ruth helped save the game almost single-handedly following the Black Sox fiasco of 1919. As late as 1998 in the home-run chase between Mark McGwire and Sammy Sosa, the ailing sport was cured of some fan discontent that still stems in part from the players' strike of 1994-95.

There will be two more seasons for baseball to surge in popularity and then another work stoppage will likely slap us hard again in the face in 2002.

There are no indications salaries will go down, not with the November contract that saw Shawn Green sign with the Los Angeles Dodgers for $84-million

J. Soohoo, Los Angeles Dodgers

Shawn Green signed six-year deal worth $84 million with L.A.

(U.S.) over six years following his trade from the Toronto Blue Jays.

Following the 2001 season, you can expect the owners to put their fists down and tell the players' association that enough is enough. Of course, the owners have pulled this stunt before but they eventually caved in to accept many of the union's demands.

The owners will want to propose a salary cap again like they have before but the players will refuse to dance. The union will do anything it can to preserve the salary-arbitration process which makes both mediocre and splendid players rich.

This is the same players' union that wouldn't go to bat for its very own employees that work in the New York office. For years, receptionists, executive assistants, etc., didn't have a pension plan. In late December of 1997, the union's executive board which also consists of players, agreed to institute a pension plan but refused to start the employees' pension retroactive to when they began employment. Some employees had been in the union's employ for 10 years and had no pension. Real cheap employer.

So we are faced with a work stoppage that will likely tear apart the 2002 season. In the meantime, we have two seasons to enjoy.

This book celebrates some of the greatest events and personalities that shaped our 20th century. Even some underdogs get their space here.

Joe Carter thought he might not get up from the ground after being swarmed by his teammates after his historic home run ended the 1993 World Series. Teammate Paul Molitor thought the same thing.

"We thought he was dead," Molitor told the author.

Kirk Gibson, Bucky Dent, Bill Mazeroski and many others talk about their role in history. We can only hope the 21st century will be as historic and entertaining.

Enjoy the book.

DANNY GALLAGHER
IN TORONTO

Chapter 1

Gibson outduels Eckersley

Before the first game of the 1988 World Series, Los Angeles Dodgers manager Tommy Lasorda told the media, "He can't do it. He just can't do it."

That 'he' was Kirk Gibson, who had helped spark the Dodgers to the National League championship over the New York Mets. Gibson's knees and legs were killing him and he just couldn't play that first night against the Oakland Athletics.

So on a balmy Saturday night with the temperature 75 degrees, Mickey (Gomer Pyle) Hatcher, the head cheerleader for the Dodgers, moved from first base to left field to replace Gibson.

And wouldn't you know it, shortly after Nancy Reagan—in a bright-red dress—threw out the first pitch, Hatcher homered to left field with Steve Sax aboard. Unbelievable. Mickey Hatcher hit a home run in the World Series! You got it.

Oakland pitcher Dave Stewart drilled Sax with a pitch to start the bottom of the first inning and home-plate umpire Doug Harvey came out to warn both benches that he would tolerate no such action anymore. Stewart then balked Sax to second and later Hatcher homered.

But that lead quickly vanished in the top of the second for Dodgers' pitcher Tim Belcher. Sandwiched around strikeouts by Walt Weiss and Dave Henderson, Glenn Hubbard singled and Belcher issued bases on balls to two batters, including Stewart, of all people. Then Jose Canseco strode to the plate.

Kirk Gibson begins his lap around the base following his memorable home run in the 1988 World Series.

"Got knocked out early," Belcher recalled close to 10 years later. "Gave up a grand slam to Canseco. He hit a slider to straight-away centre. It s-m-o-k-e-d the centre-field camera, it was a line drive, a missile. The ball didn't get anymore than 30 feet off the ground."

Ouch.

Mike Scioscia's RBI single following base hits by Mike Marshall and John Shelby made the score 4–3 in the sixth inning and that's how it was entering the bottom of the ninth inning. With Dennis Eckersley on the mound for the A's, many people at Dodger Stadium figured the game was in the bag for Oakland.

Face it: Eckersley was nearly unhittable during the regular season and the American League championship series which the A's won in four games over the Baltimore Orioles.

Scioscia popped up to start the ninth inning and Eckersley was off on the right foot. With Scioscia gone, Jeff Hamilton stepped up to the plate and pinch-hitter Mike Davis moved into the on-deck circle. When Hamilton struck out, Davis came up and Dave Anderson stood in as a potential pinch-hitter for pitcher Alejandro Pena.

At that point, Dodgers' scout Mel Didier, like many L.A. fans, headed out for the exits, figuring the game was over. Didier needed to take care of some personal business, as did his wife, before they headed to their car in the parking lot at Chavez Ravine. Nature was calling.

"I was going to the washroom from my seat at field level," Didier was saying many years later.

But lo and behold, Davis drew a walk off Eckersley. And who should come up as a pinch-hitter but Gibson, who limped up the steps of the dugout onto the field. As he would say later, Gibson had spent the entire game in the trainer's room because he was hurting so much.

After the game he told reporters, "I couldn't even do a little jog in my living room (in the morning)."

It was one of the most memorable ABs in World Series history. You all know what Gibson did. With Davis on second base following a stolen base, Gibson worked Eckersley to 3–2. Eckersley and the A's, perhaps feeling a bit cocky, decided they wouldn't walk Gibson intentionally with first base open. In came a 3–2 slider and Gibson whacked it into the right-field seats for a two-run homer to give the Dodgers an upset victory.

"I saw it on the television screen in the hallway near the washroom," Didier said. "When he hit the ball, my wife came out of the washroom. The noise was deafening. I started running toward downstairs."

"Where are you going?' Mrs. Didier asked him.

"I'll be back," her husband replied.

Didier made his way through the tunnel leading to the Los Angeles clubhouse to greet players as they were entering. He had a top-secret statement to make.

"I yelled at all of the players, 'Don't say a God-damned word to the writers about the backdoor slider. We still have a few games left in the series. Don't say anything. That's all secret.' "

Didier said his anecdote about him warning the players is something he has never, ever revealed before, although the importance of Eckersley's backdoor slider has been emphasized over and over again in the media. One little piece of evidence Didier passed on to the players before the series began had worked wonders. That at-bat, that home run will forever make a lasting impression on Didier's mind.

"It's the biggest thrill ever in my lifetime," Didier said. "In a lot of cases, the hitters don't think the pitch is coming but in this case, Gibson didn't miss. He hit it on the button. Unbelievable. With one hand."

(Up to that point of his baseball career that had spanned 45 years, Didier's biggest thrill was in 1969 when he and father Robert Irby Didier saw Mel's son, Bob, play for Atlanta.

"We were in tears during the national anthem," Mel Didier said. "My father had six sons who played pro but didn't play in the majors so we were excited that day to see Bob play.")

Gibson, hurting big time from leg and knee injuries, never played again in that series but the home run is one of the biggest in the history of the game. It was the impetus the Dodgers needed to knock off the highly rated and cocky Athletics in five games. David beat Goliath.

Mel Didier

"Yeah, that was some moment, that home run, whoo," Belcher recalled. "It was a big thrill, it was great theatre. I mean, he was hurtin'. Everybody had already written the series off in Oakland's favour anyway, that they were just going to crush us with the Bash Brothers (Mark McGwire and Canseco) and good pitching. Of course, we had good pitching, too. Eckersley was unhittable that year ... well, for a couple years. For us to snatch that game off Eckersley in the ninth, it just changed the whole complexion of the series."

In the ensuing games of the series, Canseco (0-for-18 the rest of the way) and McGwire (1-for-17) did little. A banged-up group of Dodgers, mostly short on talent, pulled off one of the biggest upsets in World Series play. It pretty much rivalled the upset victory by the New York Mets over the Orioles in the 1969 series.

"Oakland was heavily favoured," Belcher said. "I said, 'Oh well, we were severe underdogs against the Mets in the National League playoffs, too. We won that series in seven. Oakland won 104 games but one thing we did, we got momentum. We beat Eckersley and we pitched well against the meat of their order.

"We kinda had a makeshift lineup that series, a platoon system going at first with Franklin Stubbs and Mickey Hatcher. Scioscia was hurt, Gibby was out. We were kinda of banged up. It made it all worth it when you win it."

When Didier knew the Dodgers would likely be in the playoffs, he went on the road quite often to check up on Eckersley.

"I probably saw Oakland play 20 times and I picked up something Eckersley had," Didier was saying. "He'd done it on a couple of tough hitters. If the tying run was on second or third base and the count was 3–2, he'd throw the backdoor slider only to a left-handed hitter.

"When he throws that pitch, it starts out way outside and it usually ends up just on the outside corner. That year, Eckersley was wonderful. His control was unbelievable. He could knock a gnat's eye off. The times I saw him, he used the backdoor slider on George Brett of Kansas City and Wade Boggs of Boston. Boggs took a feeble swing and Brett took it for a third strike.

"Doing the advance scouting for us were Gerry Stephenson, Steve Boras and myself (Phil Regan wasn't involved, as has been reported). We had a complete booklet on the other teams. Before the World Series started, I told the guys in the clubhouse about Eckersley. I pointed my fingers at our three left-handed hitters, Gibson, Scioscia and Mike Davis.

"With my Louisiana accent, I said, 'Paaardners, remember this. When the count is 3–2 only to a left-handed hitter, he'll throw the backdoor slider.' When Gibson got to 3–2, Oakland didn't walk him, even after Davis had stolen second to put first base open. Gibson had been taking such feeble swings during the at-bat that Oakland figured there was no way he could put the ball in play. But he called time and started smiling. It meant he was relaxed. I remember the moment the ball came out of Eckersley's hand. Gibson got in a groove."

The scene after the game is something Belcher won't forget about Didier and the lesser lights of the organization.

"Probably the most memorable thing about the whole deal to me was the reaction of the team and the scouts who did the advance work on Oakland," Belcher was saying. "They were three pretty good baseball men. They'd been at it a long time. They came up with a scouting report on their entire pitching staff, a scouting report on how we should pitch their guys and so forth.

"I remember like it was yesterday when they were going over the scouting report before the series started. I can't remember if it was Gerry Stephenson or Mel Didier ... it was one of those two ... when they were going over Eckersley, they said, 'Look, bet your house on it. If the game's on the line and he's got you in a deep count, 2-2, 3-2, and you're a left-handed hitter, you can probably win the game with a home run 'cause he's going to throw you a back-door slider. He's been doing it all year.' I mean these guys watched him for weeks, scouted him the last month of the season and they got some films from the entire season.

"If you recall the at-bat and you see the highlights of the at-bat, Gibby is up there, 2-2. There's a ball, it's 3-2, and then he starts to get in the batter's box and he calls time. He steps out real quick. He said, he admitted later, that at that moment, he remembered what they said in the meeting. So, he said, 'You know, here I am up here on one leg, deep count, 3-2 situation with the one of the best relievers in the game, but I had this tidbit of information that he's going to throw a back-door slider. My only chance of hitting it is to sit on it.'

"And he did. Eckersley threw a pretty good back-door slider and Gibby reached out and hooked it to the right-field seats. And the reaction after the game was interesting because all three of those scouts were at the game. They came down to the clubhouse from the press box or owner's box or something, almost at the same time as we were coming in off the field. I was already in the clubhouse because I'd been knocked out early. There was mayhem in the clubhouse. We were jumping on each other and jumping on Gibby.

Tim Belcher

"But when those three scouts walked in, it was funny, because every player remembered that scouting report ... they were high-fiving the scouts and everything. It was awesome. That was a good moment for those three guys. I mean, you talk about, uh, the unsung heroes and the jobs behind the scenes with the advance scouts. It was important. Certainly was in that game. It really turned around the whole series. Without that one bit of information, it could have meant the whole series, really."

The move by Lasorda to insert Davis as a pinch-hitter was one lauded by Didier and other members of the organization, along with a number of Oakland players.

"Great move by Lasorda. You have to keep him credit," Didier said. "Dave Anderson (a right-handed hitter) was in the on-deck circle. He was a weak-hitting shortstop but Tommy sent Davis up. Davis had come to the Dodgers from Oakland so Oakland knew he had power. Eckersley pitched carefully to Davis and he walked. Davis steals second. Sort of perfect timing."

As Belcher said, "The other interesting thing about the home run was what preceded it ... Michael Davis, drawing off a walk off Eckersley of all people."

"Yeah," I said, "Eckersley hardly ever walked anybody."

"Yeah," Belcher continued. "I'm not certain but Michael kinda of struggled down the stretch and he was really swinging at some bad balls. But he had one heckuva at-bat and he ended up getting on base against a guy who was supposed to have as much pin-point control as anybody going at that time.

"There were so many things involved in that whole thing, things that most people would have bet against. They would have bet against Eckersley walking Michael Davis, they would have bet against Gibson hitting because he was hurting, they would have bet against Gibson hitting the pitch out for a home run. It certainly turned the series around.

"A great series. Wow. We did the little things right. Pitched well. It carried us a long way. If Davis doesn't draw that walk, Gibby doesn't get to the plate. When you draw a walk off Dennis Eckersley ... like, he walked, like, three guys (11 to be exact) all year. Unbelievable. There were so many weird, really extraordinary things that happened that helped make that moment possible. It all made it a special moment ... the scouts, Mike Davis, Gibby. There was a nice hook to skip, too ... I would've taken the loss," Belcher said, as he laughed.

"I was in the back of the press box, thinking the game was over and I was wondering what I was going to write about," recalled Ross Newhan, a long-time writer for the Los Angeles Times. "Then Gibson put the ball into the air."

Newhan knew what he was writing about. So did the rest of the press box. Gibson had sat in the clubhouse out of sight most of the game and nobody but him knew if he could even make a pinch-hit appearance.

"On game day, it was ugly," Gibson told me years later. "My left knee had torn muscle and there was ligament damage to my right knee. I tried to walk and it was a real ugly, ugly, ugly feeling. During the game, I put the pillows under my leg and sucked it up. I tried to jog and I said, 'Oh, my god.' It was the ugliest, most horrible feeling. Before the game, I had two cortisone shots in both knees."

The way Gibson tells the story, it was a shock to Lasorda when Gibson instructed him via a batboy that he would go up and pinch-hit.

"Tommy looked around at me and said, 'What?! Are you kidding?" Gibson recalled.

> "On game day, it was ugly. My left knee had torn muscle and there was ligament damage to my right knee. I tried to walk and it was a real ugly, ugly, ugly feeling. Before the game, I had two cortisone shots in both knees. It was the ugliest, most horrible feeling."
>
> — Kirk Gibson

Naturally, Lasorda wasn't going to argue so he put Gibson in to hit.

"I was so excited," Gibson recalled. "How it happened ... the whole moment ... I sat and visualized that moment. I thought about it in my mind. I mentally thought I could make a contribution. I had the whole game to think about it. Visualization is very important, to visualize a great moment. I was hurt but it didn't matter.

"I was relaxed up there. I was locked in. I wasn't giving in. The count was 0-2 and I went into my emergency stance. I couldn't hit his fastballs. I fouled them off. I was hoping to get him to 3-2. We'd been told in the scouting report that if the count got to 3-2, he'd throw a back-door slider. When the count went to 3-2, Eckersley came to the stretch but I called time. He threw the pitch and I pulled it. It was an important hit and helped us win the trophy."

Dodgers' shortstop Alfredo Griffin recalled the scene as Gibson limped to the plate. Griffin was taken out of the game as Davis pinch-hit for him.

"Everyone was tense and quiet," Griffin said. "As soon as Gibby hit the ball, he changed everyone's face. Oh, it was amazing. He lifted us up, picked us up, gave us a lot of confidence. We were underdogs all the way down since the playoffs started. For me, the key thing was beating the Mets in the playoffs. When we beat them, I knew we'd be in good shape. Gibby limped around the bases, he got home and it looked like we'd won the World Series right there. I said, 'Hey, wait a minute, we just started the series.'"

Were Gibson's mates and Oakland players surprised Gibson got up there to pinch-hit?

"Ah, yes and no," Belcher said. "We knew he was hurtin'. He had knee problems and hamstring problems the whole year. He was definitely hurtin'. But we also knew that if he thought he could get up there and swing, he would."

Oakland slugger Dave Parker, who had collected three hits earlier in the game before being replaced, was walking back into the

Mark McGwire played for Oakland in the 1988 World Series.

dugout after taking a shower in the clubhouse. He had an eerie hunch, a premonition.

"Gibson was dragging on one leg to the plate and I knew, standing and watching him come to the plate, that he was going to hit a home run," Parker told me. "There was just something that told me. It was a Hollywood script. It didn't surprise me. I felt it. When he hit it, I turned around and walked back to the clubhouse.

"Some people said the Dodgers didn't have a chance in hell to beat us. We had a dominant, strong team. You know what hurt us? They played a seven-game series with New York and we sat for a week. The best team didn't win."

Looking back, McGwire said Gibson's home run "took the sails out of our ship."

"I made a comment not too long ago ... I think the biggest thing that hurt us in the '88 World Series was walking Mike Davis to allow Gibson to come to the plate," McGwire said. "There were two out, we had a one-run lead. It was, like, no room to put anyone on base. We threw four straight balls to Mike Davis and then, all of a sudden, up comes Kirk Gibson. It was a slider that was supposed to be away and it ended up over the middle of the plate. It was the only ball that he had a chance to hit and he hit it. It turned out, to this day, to probably be one of the most memorable home runs in World Series history.

"Not following the National League as much, I don't think we knew how extensive his injuries were but I mean, he was a gamer. They just beat us basically in everything. We were one of the most powerful teams in the game, they had a bunch of no-names. They had Mickey Hatcher (McGwire was laughing when he mentioned him). They had a bunch of guys who aren't playing today.

"If you want to match up, we totally dominated them as far as match-ups. But you know how baseball is, it doesn't mean anything in match-ups. You have to go out there and play between the lines."

So very true. The Dodgers played over the heads and the A's underachieved. As McGwire lamented somewhat, the A's weren't able to use a designated hitter in the first two games of the series.

"Incredible," Canseco told me about Gibson's homer. "That knocked the wind out of our sails. We thought we had the game won. I'd hit the grand slam and Eckersley comes in and you figure the game's over. I remember playing right field and Gibson hits it and when I saw it, it looked like a breaking ball down and away and he turned and hooked it.

"When I saw him hit it, I said, 'I've got a play on this ball.' Then, I take two steps back and I said, 'Shit, this ball is going out.' The ball is going over my head and I'm saying, 'Oh, my God.' That flattened us. That's what helped them win the series because they were struggling."

Mark McGwire

Back in 1997, Gibson's home run was voted the most celebrated sports moment in the long sports history of Los Angeles. Not much argument there.

"It was theatre," Belcher re-iterated. "NBC was doing the series and the next night, they did a comparison. They had clips of The Natural where Robert Redford (character was Roy Hobbs) hit a home run. Then it flashed to Gibby and flashed to the movie."

The makers of the movie changed the script somewhat from the book written by Bernard Malamud. In the ending of the book, Hobbs struck out in a crucial at-bat. In the movie, he homered.

"Have you seen a more important home run hit than Gibson's?" I asked Belcher.

"No, none with the same kind of meaning," Belcher replied. "I mean, that's the world stage, that's the World Series. Probably the one that would come close would be Mike Scioscia's homer in the NL championship series in game 4 against Dwight Gooden of the Mets. I started that game and went back to the hotel early and watched it there. The homer tied it and sent the game into extra innings. It was a huge home run, an absolute bomb."

Jose Canseco

McGwire admits to having heard all about the backdoor-slider theory but as he said, "All I know is that Dennis threw it right over the middle. It wasn't where he wanted it. You know what, after something like that, some guys would fold. Actually, Dennis' career was just starting as a stopper in 1988. See what he has done since then. He's been one of the best stoppers in the game. Quite remarkable what he has done considering what has happened to him. He hasn't had an easy road during his career. It's been an amazing 20-plus years."

> "It was something awesome, man, walking across that field. They were going apeshit and they weren't clapping for me. Yeah, it's the total, ultimate walk-off," Dennis Eckersley said about the aftermath of allowing Gibson's homer.

Dennis Eckersley was hurt more by a 1992 home run by Robbie Alomar.

Eckersley told me the home run is a pain, "just something that will never go away."

"But that's okay because so many good things have happened since that time," Eckersley said. "It was great for the game at the time, not for me, but for the game. It was nice to get back to the World Series the next year and the next year. That pain didn't last as long. I was just really happy to be there in that moment and time. It was something awesome, man, walking off that field. They were going apeshit and they weren't clapping for me," he said, chuckling.

"It's quite an experience to go through. Yeah, it's the total, ultimate walk-off. It bothered me for a couple days. I was dream-walking anyway sort of. My career had started to get better. I was back on top. I was feeling real fortunate to be where I was at the time and not saying, 'Oh, fuck, isn't this awful?' I was saying, 'I've got it going in my career again.'

"I threw him a back-door breaking ball on 3-2," Eckersley said, just emphasizing what everybody else was saying. "We weren't even supposed to be throwing him breaking balls. He said he was looking for one that he got the tip from a scout. The way he swung at it, he looked like shit but he's so strong.

"That's the only ball he could hit, if you think about it. He took a cockshot at it. I gave him the only pitch he could hit out. It was one moment in time for him, you know. It's something he'll probably always be remembered for but it's not something I'll always be remembered for because I did so many other good things. They said I throw a lot of 3-2, back-door breaking balls, right? I don't know how they found out I just did it on 3-2. He (Didier) might have seen one game where I threw a 3-2 breaking ball. How many 3-2 counts do you get if you only walk eight guys a year (11 walks as indicated before)? Believe me, I don't get pulled (to right) that often."

Eckersley then assessed the Davis at-bat, admitting he wasn't up to snuff.

"That was a bad one. Yeah, I was pitching him kinda carefully," Eck said. "Yeah, because I played with him the year before. I knew he had some pop. You looked on-deck and there was nothing there. I forget who was on-deck. Dave Anderson, somebody. I tried to be too cute. The walk hurt more than anything.

"I remember Doug Harvey was the umpire. I started the all-star game in Montreal in 1982 and he was behind the fuckin' plate. I didn't win that game either. I don't know why but he sticks out in my mind. No big deal."

Tony Phillips of the A's said Gibson's home run didn't by itself sink Oakland but instead, he praised the Dodgers for their execution.

""We didn't lose because of that but we never recovered," Phillips said. "We lost because everything they did was right. Everytime they used ... the hit and run ... it worked. Every move Lasorda made, it worked. Mickey Hatcher was hot as a firecracker. Wasn't he the MVP in the Series? A lot of guys had a great series."

When he was asked if he was surprised Gibson came up to pinch hit, Phillips said, "Not at all .. the way he played against the Mets in the NLCS ... the way he played hurt. He knows his fuckin' heart. His fuckin' nuts are as big as this building. His heart is tremendous. I learned that by playing with him in Detroit."

Oakland catcher Terry Steinbach doesn't think, either, that the home run sunk the A's.

"I don't know if it was demoralizing, that's a pretty harsh word," Steinbach said. "Was it a big hit? Yeah, it ended up being a big hit for the Dodgers but the point was we did have three more games to play after that. With the calibre of team we were, we should have been able to overcome something like that. We had other games to play. We just didn't have a lot of post-season experience.

"The thing is that everybody misses the point. They looked at Gibson, then they'd refer to Eck. They'd say, 'Boy, Eck gave it up to Gibson and that's why we lost.' But no one ever thinks about the situation before that when we should never have walked Michael Davis.

"Eck walked Michael Davis and now a lot of your closers in the game don't know how to hold runners on at first. Davis stole second. Now, there's two out in a one-run game. Even if Gibson only gets a hit, it's a tie game. A home run is icing on the game. The situation intensified because we walked Davis. With the success Dennis had all year, it wasn't like we said, 'Be careful.' It wasn't like we said, 'Don't do this.'

"Tip your hat to Davis for drawing the walk. Eck wasn't trying to walk him. It just happened. It was a one-run game. Eck was in the situation many times before with the number of saves he had that year. He didn't want to throw it down the middle. He wanted to make quality pitches as well. Michael Davis had a good at-bat."

And what about that back-door slider, Terry?

"Hindsight is always 20-20," he said. "I mean, he hit it great, he hit it good. But it wasn't like it was just a hanger. It was a pretty decent pitch. He easily could have popped that ball up to second or grounded to first. It was just one of those things."

Seven years following his famous home run, Gibson tried to use it as an inspiration to break out of a horrific slump he was enduring while he was with the Tigers.

"A fan had given him a tape of the home run," former Tiger Travis Fryman said. "Obviously, he had his own tape at home. One day very early in the afternoon, there was hardly anybody in the clubhouse and he plugged in this tape to look at it. He was trying to draw on some positives. The way he spoke about it in the first person, it gave you an awesome feeling.

"Within a few weeks, he retired. The Tigers, at the same time,

14

were going through the changes and really struggling in the first half. They started to make trades. They traded David Wells and Mike Henneman. It was apparent we were rebuilding. Gibby was playing through a very serious shoulder injury and he wasn't playing well. It was not a very enjoyable situation to be in. His retirement was done very quietly. He told Alan Trammell and Sparky Anderson. I didn't know he was going to retire."

Gibson had signed a free-agent contract with the Dodgers in the fall of 1987 and arrived in Dodgerland during spring training in 1988 a fresh face in a sea of happy-go lucky teammates. This was a team based in the shadow of Hollywood and the sun, a team rich in tradition, a team playing in a laid-back atmosphere where Lasorda routinely hugged players.

Turns out Gibson was going to kick butt. He was a dragon, who brought a breathing-fire, no-nonsense passion to the clubhouse and practices ... yes ... even during spring training.

"Gibson basically was the type who said to forget golf clubs and fishing poles," Didier said.

Gibson's new buddies knew he was an intense player but they didn't know how intense. They soon discovered that they shouldn't play games with him.

Dodgers reliever Jesse Orosco, another new face and a jokester wherever his uniform takes him, decided he would raise the ire of Gibson by placing eye-black inside his cap. Gibson was incensed after he discovered he had unknowingly wiped the goo all over himself.

At first, Gibson didn't know who had fashioned the dirty deed but he dashed away to see Lasorda and complain. Lasorda tried to calm Gibson down, saying he shouldn't take things so seriously. Gibson would have nothing to do with Lasorda's explanation and insisted on meeting with his teammates over the matter. Lasorda relented, albeit reluctantly, to allow Gibson to speak his mind.

"Orosco? He didn't know me," Gibson told me. "Basically, he got unfocused while I was very focused. The Dodgers had finished in fourth place a few times and there was a lot of screwing around. I was the first guy on the field stretching and running and getting locked in.

"Then they pull that crap. They said they were trying to make me feel welcome, that they were trying to have fun. Well, I talked to them in the clubhouse and told them that winning is fun. I challenged them right there to set a team goal. I told them all, 'I'll take you all on right now (nobody volunteered).' It turns out Jesse and I became good friends. I was hard-nosed. Baseball is a team sport. You have to have 25 guys to set the same goal. It's not how many wins a pitcher can get or if you go 1-for-3 at the plate."

Around reporters, Gibson could be just as nasty. During the Dodgers-Mets' series that took place before the World Series in '88, I ventured over to Gibson's stall after an off-day practice and asked him if he would play that night despite the fact he was really hurting. It was a question he had heard many times before and he was upset.

"That's a fucking stupid question?" Gibson replied.

When I told Gibson that yarn years later, he chuckled and said, "That sounds like me."

Belcher, who is about as intense as anyone in the game, welcomed Gibson to the Dodgers' fold.

"It was just his attitude that helped us," Belcher said. "Dodger Stadium and the Dodger organization are such a great place to play, such a fun place to play for players. Everything's first class. You get spoiled by that. Everyone gets in a kind of lull every now and then. You'd say, 'Okay, we'll win tomorrow.'

"Gibby came in with more of an abrasive attitude. 'You know, screw the plush atmosphere and all the perks. Let's win. The hell with all that other stuff.' We needed that at the time."

Know what? The intangibles provided by Gibson in '88 convinced the voters, the members of the Baseball Writers Association of America, that he should be the NL's MVP. He drove in only 76 runs but he scored 106 and did a lot of little things, like scoring from second on a passed ball. Long before the voting took place, people such as Montreal Expos manager Buck Rodgers were saying Gibson should be the MVP.

"He didn't drive in a lot of runs and there's a lot said about that, the fact that he was MVP," Belcher said. "I think the people who had MVP ballots that year took a little heat for voting him MVP. But to me, that represents the true essence of what the award should be. It's not a statistical competition. It's for the most valuable player. And he was. He was more valuable to our team than any other player in the whole league. He did the little things. You just don't capture those kinds of abilities in every player. They come around once in a while."

Said Gibson, "I loved being the guy who stepped up. A lot of guys would shy away from those situations. I loved to be there when everyone else didn't want to be. When I would go for home from second, I wasn't thinking of getting thrown out."

Underneath the unshaven, stand-offish, grim-looking face, Gibson had another side to him, Belcher said.

16

"He was no-nonsense but hmmmmm, he was a real pussycat, you know," Belcher said. "He had that scowl and that rough look when he was on the field ... the hair all messed up ... the thick beard. A pussycat, though. I wouldn't back him into a corner and challenge him to a fight but if you really get down to a personal level, he was a pussycat kind of guy."

When Gibson rounded the bases, he was the epitome of a thoroughbred race horse.

"Oh, yeah, the fastest caucasian I've ever played with, no question," Belcher said. "For a big guy, too, he could really run. He wasn't built for speed. Gibby was an outside linebacker. You don't think he's fast when you look at him but he could really run. He had a really good understanding of how to run properly. He had the proper technique. He worked with a lot of track coaches."

Fryman saw that fierce competitor in Gibson, too.

"Gibby is more outspoken," Fryman said. "Other guys played with the same intensity but demonstrated it in different ways. But he carries an air about him, which comes with him because he's such a demonstrative player. So he certainly carries a presence, a presence that keeps a lot of guys in check.

"Obviously, he's a very intense competitor, very prepared in everything he does. He practised with the same intensity with which he played. He's a very intelligent person. That's one thing that really struck me. I never thought he was stupid before I played with him. But when you play with him, I was struck that he was a voracious leader. He was a very intelligent man, a great teammate. If you play hard, he respects you. If you don't, well, you're like a lot of guys, you don't have a lot of respect for that.' If you play hard like him, he will respect you. If you don't, you're on his shit list."

In his autobiography appropriately entitled Bottom of the Ninth, Gibson talked of perseverance. He talked of The Beast. That's been the theme of his life ... to play hard, to try and get to the World Series.

"In the end, we won the big war. It was a very special moment," Gibson told me. "Winning the World Series was the goal, not hitting .300 and driving in 100 runs. You set your goals high. I was a World Series champion two times. I loved to be there when everybody else didn't want to be.

"When we'd get beat and a guy went 4-for-4 and he'd be happy, I'd say, 'Asshole, shut the fuck up.' If we lost, I was the orniest son-of-o-bitch in the clubhouse. People get the misconception that athletes are spoiled prima donnas and things come easy. I had some ability. I didn't have Ken Griffey Jr. ability. I pooled my resources."

Kirk Gibson

Gibson has been pooling his resources these days away from the field managing his ranches, stocks and bonds and checking out real-estate deals. He's also a broadcaster with the Tigers, an outspoken one at that.

Gibson also plays non-contact but intense recreational hockey in the Detroit area and if he had become a pro player on the ice, he would have been a tough dude like Eric Lindros or former badboy John Ferguson, who detested the opposition and didn't want to associate with them either. Gibson has attended many Detroit Red Wings' games and has taken some fighting lessons from Red Wings' enforcer Joey Kocur.

Eckersley vs. Gibson pitch by pitch was a seven-minute adventure

Fastball — fouled off.
Fastball — fouled off.
Fastball — fouled off.
Fastball — ball one.
Fastball — fouled off.
Fastball — ball two.
Curveball inside — ball three.
Back-door slider — homer to right.

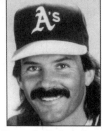
Dennis Eckersley

"If someone drills me into the boards, I return the favour," Gibson said about his play in the league. "I'd be a mean bastard if I played pro hockey. I didn't like talking to the other players on the other teams. Late in my career, I mellowed and that's why I quit. Hockey's a great game. Lindros is an unbelievable talent. I love him."

Is there a place in the Hall of Fame for an inspirational leader like Gibson? Is there a spot in Cooperstown for someone who hit a dramatic World Series homer? Probably not. The hall is meant for players who dominated the game for at least 10 years in statistical fashion. Intangibles aren't considered by the writers.

"The Hall of Fame is no big deal. It's not sour grapes. My Hall of Fame is my four kids," Gibson said. "The Hall of Fame isn't set up for guys like me. It's set up for guys like Wade Boggs.

"There are some worthy guys who have gone into the hall but you know what, there have been guys who have gone in there and their teammates said, 'What did he do?' I've seen that asshole,

Boggs, go up there with men on second and third with a guy like Nolan Ryan pitching and he'd take a cockshot swing and try to get a walk. Boggs would just hand it off to the next guy. He'd want his average to stay at .344 instead of seeing it go down. That's why I'm personally slandering him. There aren't many money players like I was."

In April of '98 in his role of a Tigers' broadcaster, Gibson roasted Boggs again: "He never did anything. He's not a team player. His only claim to fame is he got a walk with the bases loaded to win a World Series game (for the Yankees)."

Ten years following the infamous backdoor-slider , Eckersley quit baseball at age 43 after passing Hoyt Wilhelm to pitch in 1,071 games. Gibson's home run, get this, isn't the biggest disappointment of Eck's career.

A home run he coughed up to Roberto Alomar of the Toronto Blue Jays in the 1992 American League championship series stung him more. The A's were leading the game 6-1 at the time and the Jays came back to win the game, the series and later the World Series. That was the year Eckersley recorded 51 saves, sported a 7-1 record and a puny 1.91 ERA. Whew. Those stats prompted writers to vote him the winner of both the Cy Young and MVP awards in the same season. Not often that happens.

"Oh yeah, that home run hurt more because I felt more responsible for that playoff," Eckersley told me. "I had such a great year that year and that burst ny bubble. It took away from getting those awards because of the pain of the Alomar thing. Oh, I was in tears. I felt so responsible. We still had a chance to win that game. If we'd won that fuckin' game, then I'm off the hook, right? It wouldn't have mattered if he had gone deep, if we had won and they lost.

"That just tied the series. The Jays were all over me because I was pointing at somebody and punching out somebody the inning before. Well, fuck, there were men on second and third with two out and the score was 6-4. They were coming back because the score was 6-1. That was a b-i-g, major out. That really hurt more than anything, that Alomar home run."

Yet, Eckersley said, "Getting the awards mean everything and getting the Cy Young and MVP in he same year is, you know, remarkable. I had a better year in 1990 but I didn't get shit."

Chapter 2

Carter hits one for Hollywood

When Joe Carter touched home plate about 11:40 p.m. on October 23, 1993, he was assaulted.

You know how it is when one wins a league championship, a World Series, people go crazy. You don't just pat people on the back, you tackle, you jump on bodies, you jump on someone's shoulders. You mean well but you don't think of the possible consequences.

"Joe was kind of at the bottom of the pile," recalled one of his teammates, Paul Molitor. "When we cleared the pile, Joe was at the bottom and he didn't move. We thought maybe it had killed him. Finally, he let go one of those Joe smiles and we lifted him to his feet. Then we jolted him to our shoulders."

Carter recalls that his mind had gone blank on the ground with little room for breathing. His Toronto Blue Jays' teammates were jumping on him and he was trying to survive the pounding.

"I almost passed out," Carter told the author years later. "I hit home plate and I got tackled. Your mind goes completely blank. When they picked me up, the first thing I did was just look up and say: 'Thank you, Jesus.' I mean, I give him all the honour. Without him, I wouldn't be doing anything. He's our creator and he's been there for me. That's the only thing I could think of. After that, it was mind boggling."

Yes, it was something else. Carter had hit one of the most mind boggling home runs in major-league history when he belted a three-run shot to win the 1993 World Series for the Jays.

Carter went up to the plate to face Mitch Williams of the Philadelphia Phillies not feeling any butterflies. He claims he wasn't nervous at all. Rickey Henderson was on first, Molitor was at third.

"No, you know, I'm more nervous sitting on the bench than when I am at the plate," Carter told me. "I even hate watching sports on television, as far as championship basketball or something ... a baseball game, the World Series ... because I know I can't do anything about it.

"So from that standpoint, I'd rather be up there facing a pitcher rather than sitting back and waiting and seeing what's going to happen. It's like being in control. I was thinking about a lot of things in that at-bat. I was thinking about my wife and my family because when you come up in a situation like that, they're nervous, they're holding hands. And I'm saying, 'Wow.'

"My parents were there. My father-in-law. They're nervous. My wife is nervous. I'm saying, 'This is fun (he was laughing).' I knew they were more nervous than I was. I think the only nervous time probably is your first at-bat in the World Series. I mean you're trying to get that first hit. I mean, I've played baseball so long. It comes natural and that's the good thing about it."

Then the conversation switched to the actual at-bat, one of the most historic in the game. Williams threw two fastballs that were "way away", according to Joltin' Joe.

"He got behind 2-0 and I said, 'No way was I swinging at 2-0.' I took a fastball down the middle of the plate, which is what usually happens anyway," Carter was saying.

"On the 2-1, he threw me a slider ... I hadn't faced Mitch, man, since his days with Texas which was four to five years earlier ... I saw him a lot on TV. I saw him face a lot of our guys but I never got the chance. I was never a guy up when he was pitching.

"He threw me a slider and you know, I lost it because at the time, Mickey Morandini was playing right behind second base. And as a hitter, you always move the umpires because I don't like the ball coming in out of someone's uniform or someone being right there (with the pitch on top of the hitter).

"Mitch was pitching from the side ... he threw right out of his uniform and I swung badly because I lost where the ball was. That's when I said, 'Man, I gotta sit back. I can't really think about pulling the ball. I gotta make sure I see the ball.' That's when it was 2-2. I said, 'I have to make sure I see the ball. Don't worry about yanking it. Just see the ball and put the ball in play somewhere.' "

> I wasn't thinking of hooking it. If I'm trying to hook it, I'm going to hit that ball foul every time, without a doubt. I was thinking of putting the ball in play." Joe Carter on his celebrated homer.

Carter was saying that 90 out of 100 times, he'll hook a fastball foul if it's down and in. The ball was outside and down in the strike zone. It was a ball and Carter was glad Williams threw it outside because it made me concentrate even that much more.

"If I'm trying to hook it, I'm going to hit that ball foul every time, without a doubt," Carter said. "I made sure I saw that next one. Hitting a fastball is just reaction but I had to make sure it was my strength. I wasn't thinking of hooking it. I was thinking of putting the ball in play."

By staying back and looking at the ball, Carter reasoned that he was able to keep the 2-2 pitch fair.

"I mean it wasn't ... people look ... it wasn't a bad pitch, I mean, it was a fastball down and in but it was like a cutter because he was worried about Rickey (Henderson) at third base," Carter said. "It was more like a slide-step. It wasn't his full motion where he turns.

"He did the slide-step and as a hitter, I like people who do that slide-step because it's almost like a timing mechanism because you know they're not going to rear back and come forth. They have to do everything a lot quicker so it gets your momentum going, at least for me."

When he hit the ball, the first thing Carter did was keep his head down and when he looked up, all he saw was lights, a bank of lights. He never saw the ball until he took three or four steps out of the batter's box. Phillies catcher Darren Daulton was to tell me, too, that he felt the same way because he was wincing with his eyes using his mitt as a shield, trying to locate the ball.

This photo of bunny-hopping Joe Carter celebrating his famous home run to end the 1993 World Series was snapped by Rick Eglinton of the Toronto Star with a 500 mm. lens on a Nikon F3 camera. The shot earned him a National Newspaper Award for best sports photo of 1993. The photo, as Eglinton explained, was fashioned with a manual focus and captured three "subtle" moments. "His mouth is open, the helmet is off and his arms are back," the photographer said. "That's the only photo that I know of that shows the helmet coming off. Nobody else got that. I got three frames of him in that situation and the first frame was the best."

23

That's when you saw Phillies' left-fielder Pete Incaviglia turn his back to you. He stopped to look. Bye-bye, home run.

"Pete kind of like stopped," Carter said. "That's when I noticed ... I'd picked the ball up and I said: 'That ball is out of there.' I said, 'No way.' I never thought about home run. It was just moreorless, put the ball in play. And look at what happened. As I was rounding the bases, I touched first base. If I could do cartwheels, I would've done cartwheels on the bases. That's how happy I felt. That's what I felt like doing but as a kid, I never learned how to do cartwheels (like Ozzie Smith).' "

All Carter could think of as he rounded the bases was how electrifying the moment was. He may not have been doing cartwheels but he sure did the bunny-hop routine more than a few times as he made his way to home plate.

"Man, I was looking around, looking at the crowd, thinking of my wife, my father and mother, father-in-law, sister. Wow, when I was down on the ground and watching my teammates, the biggest thrill of any athlete in a team sport is coming through for your team. We won it, we won it. I didn't realize that the season was over."

Back in 1984, Carter had a special day against Ron Guidry of the Yankees while playing for the Cleveland Indians as a rookie. Carter tagged Guidry for a grand slam and later added a two-run shot for a six-RBI day. It left him in shock.

"I was walking around, saying, 'Were the bases really loaded? Did this really happen?' I felt the same thing there in the World Series. 'Did this really happen? I mean this has to be a dream.' When I touched home plate after the World Series game, it was like, 'Wow.' I just said, 'Thank you, Jesus.' It was like a special moment. Inky (Incavgilia) always says I have goosebumps thinking about it. He's always making me think about it.

"After my big day against Guidry, I couldn't wait until after the game to call my mom and dad. 'Hey, I hit two homers and had six RBI.' That was a career day and off a guy like Guidry, who is no slouch."

Since the home run off Williams, Carter had told Williams that the pitch for a homer was "a good one." Carter has no criticism for Williams, saying "Mitch is a great guy. He handled it (aftermath) good. The fans in Philly thought he lost the whole World Series. That's not true. You don't lose the whole World Series. As a team, you win, as a team, you lose. You go from goat to hero. He was more or less the goat. First time I saw him after that, he was with California and he played hero. He said, "how come you didn't send a limo for me at the airport?' I said, "I would have but I didn't know you were with the Angels.' I hadn't kept up where he was at. The home run isn't something I brag about. You can be really good and really bad the next day. I don't try to get too high if you have a good game and don't get too low, if you have a bad game. I could very easily have been in the situation where I struck out or hit into a double play. It's not something I want to gloat over.'

In ensuing seasons, Carter used the famous blast as a motiva-tion, a flashback, a thought process, an inspiration. Rarely does a day go by that someone doesn't mention the home run to him.

One of Carter's nephews watched the game in Dallas with Tony Dorsett (ex-NFL star) and Dorsett remarked, "To be able to see that, to witness something like that. Not everyone can see it live."

Said Carter, "When I heard Tony say that, that kind of topped off everything. That was icing on the cake right there."

Kirk Gibson's home run off Dennis Eckersley in Game 1 of the 1988 World Series was a blast that has always impressed Carter.

"His was probably more classic because you had the best re-liever in baseball, you have a guy that's hurt, can't walk," Carter said. "What people don't forget is the guy who set it up was Mike Davis. He walked and stole second. You always have to have a prelude to it. Mike gave Kirk the chance."

Funny thing happened to Carter following his home run ... the celebrations were almost over by the time he made it to the players' lounge in the Jays' clubhouse.

"The only thing I hated was that I missed all the celebrations in the clubhouse because I was doing interviews," he said. "Champagne opened up on the World Series trophy but I was taken away to the interview room, then I did interviews on the field.

"I came back in to shower and everyone was gone back in the back room with their families talking. I said to myself; 'Man, I missed everything.' It was anti-climatic. From that standpoint, after the World Series in 1992 in Atlanta, we had a lot more fun. (Jays' president) Paul Beeston rented the whole downstairs at the Hotel Nigro. It was a huge party. It was noisy. Old guys were dancing, young guys were dancing. Dave Winfield was dancing, even (boring, staid) John Olerud was dancing. That was fun. But here, after winning the '93 Series, we went upstairs in a small club, it was moreorless eat a little and go home. I got home at 4 and I was up at 7 because I had an interview on Good Morning America."

And just so you will know, Carter wasn't hung over the next day. He was stone sober because he was never a drinker.

"Don't drink at all," he said. "I've never had a beer, no drinks, no drugs, no smokes, no nothing. I have always been the type to stay away from that. Hal McRae (former Kansas City Royals' player) was telling me when I was younger that I would start drinking.

"Because when you've been in the big leagues a few years, you'll drink," he recalled McRae saying. "I said, 'No, I won't. I don't have a taste for it.' I saw him three or four years later and he kept saying, 'Wait till next year, wait till next year. Wait until you have a great year. Wait until you have a bad year. Wait when you play every day with all that strain.' I said, 'Hal, I still haven't had a drink.' He said; 'Hey, you win the bet. I'll buy you a drink.' I said' Yeah, right?' "

In the aftermath, Carter thinks his home run wasn't played up as much as it should have been. Baseball doesn't promote itself as much as basketball which is adored by kids, according to Carter.

"You see basketball players in every commercial, they're on television, everywhere, billboards, ads, everywhere. Baseball's not like that," Carter said. "You have 28 teams with a 25-man roster that's going up and down every other week. I mean, you got to go out and market guys. You got guys like Ken Griffey (he finally got marketed). That should have been done a long time ago. For something like what I did ... I don't always look for publicity. When something like that is done very special, then why not play it up? I mean, it's not every day you see that. You want to get impressions in people's minds, to get some excitement in the game. If you don't market anything, it's not going to be there."

Carter did do commercials in Canada for McDonald's and the Ontario Milk Marketing Board.

"The milk marketing board thing ... I was in a huge scene

oversized and it made me look like a little kid. That little kid with the beard. That was fun. I enjoyed that because I'm still a kid. I'm a b-i-g kid," Carter said. "You see yourself on TV. My kids loved the commercials."

When it came right down to it, Carter could've attracted more commercials but he didn't push for it that much, especially in the winter months following his historic homer.

"A lot of it had to do with me," Carter said. "Because in the off-season, I don't like doing too much. After the World Series, it was close to November and we started playing in February at spring training. You're talking about eight-and-a-half, good months. And now, I've got two to three months at home with my kids, whom I haven't seen much of. Probably the biggest reason I was happy about the home run was that I could go home and see my kids. I had not seen them.

"I could've done something every week as far as speaking engagements. I had agents from California calling me and telling me they could get me bit parts in movies and that. 'We can put your name out there.' But they wanted me to pay them first to go out and solicit advertising and solicit deals for me. I said, 'If you can do all of that, go ahead and do it and I'll pay you the commission. But don't have me pay first and then say: 'Well, I couldn't get anything for you' and it's doing to cost you $80,000. So I said, thanks, but no thanks.' "

Carter said the home run didn't change him but it changed the way people saw him. He got noticed a lot more. It used to be that he would say, 'Hi, I'm Joe Carter, Toronto Blue Jays.' But then it was 'I'm Joe.' They say: 'Oh, yeah, you hit the home run.' They automatically know now. You lose a little of your privacy but I'm still not a very private person. I like to be out in public. I'm not a prisoner in my own world. I still got out and do things, go eat anywhere I want to eat and not worry about my privacy."

From the viewpoint of the Phillies, the home run was predictably tough to swallow.

"It was a tough moment," said Larry Bowa, then the third-base coach. "We felt we had the momentum on our side going into that inning. Anytime you have a guy like Joe up there in a situation like that where he can drive in a run to beat you or tie you, you're in a little trouble because he's a clutch hitter. He can

---

Joe Carter's historic homer was on October 23, 1993.

Joe Carter posed for photos after being named a baseball analyst for CTV SportsNet games involving the Blue Jays.

drive in big runs. With Mitch on the mound, pitching behind hitters as often as he did, it's not a real-good situation to be in.

"In the game of baseball, you can feel it when momentum switches. We took the lead, you could feel it. It just vanished into thin air. You had it in your hands and you had it taken away from you real quick."

For Molitor, who had never won a World Series prior to '93, well, this exhilaration was basically next to none. It was a very emotional time for him. Finally, he had won something significant.

"Personally, I can't really come close to finding a home run or a moment in a game that compares to that moment," the very eloquent Molitor told me. "For so many reasons personally ... it was my 16th season ... I'd never been on a championship team ... it was my first year on a new club. It culminated a year of transition for me in the most dramatic of fashions.

"Being on base when it was hit and watching a guy hit a home run to win the World Series is pretty unique. It's the second time it has been done. It's the first time after the team trailed. To be part of that, to be actually there, just brought on so many emotions in such a short period of time. Then circling the bases, joining the celebration at home plate. ... the pileup, the hugs ... it seemed like we were out there for a long time and then I looked at the tape and it wasn't really that long. It just seemed like everything at that particular moment was lingering. The pitch and the noise of the dome was just penetrating."

And because this was Molitor's first World Series win after spending so many years in Milwaukee, well, most of the players and manager Cito Gaston sought him out for hugs after they had finished their assault on Carter.

Molitor shed more than a few tears that night in gratitude. His embrace of Gaston is one moment that seems to stand out on videotapes of the event. The tears welling in his eyes, the face contorting into a grimace of happiness. Very touching for anyone who was watching.

"It was probably my most emotional moment on the field," Molitor said. "I think the only other time I ever had a tear in my eye was when my hitting streak (37 games) ended in 1987. I got a curtain call by the fans in Milwaukee and I remember coming out with tears in my eyes. I saw my family's eyes in the stands and they were all crying.

"It kind of hit me. That was a different type of emotion, to be given that type of appreciation by the fans. I often think that if we were winning 5-1 (in the World Series) and we had gone on to win that game 5-1 or 5-2 or 6-1, I think the celebration would have been a little bit different as far as emotion.

"I felt it coming on but with the dramatics of the game and the tenseness of that last inning, the way it ended, it caused more of an instanteous reaction than if we'd coasted in with that 5-1 win, not that it was better or worse. The way it ended, it caused more emotion."

Daulton says losing that series was the "most disappointing moment of my life."

"Anytime it's a home run, it's not a good pitch. It was down and in. We were just trying to work both sides of the plate," Daulton said. "Mitch was a little low on bullets. He had pitched a lot of for us. He'd saved 43 saves for us. He probably didn't have the stuff that he had earlier in the year so I don't think he was throwing as hard in the playoffs and the series as he was capable of.

"I never saw it off his (Carter's) bat. I just happened to be on that plane coming in. I was kinda watching him and everyone else because there were runners on base and I was anticipating a play at home plate. Then I saw everyone's attention going to left field and I saw the ball go over the fence and I knew the season was over right then."

Phillies skipper Jim Fregosi, who became the Jays' manager in time for the 1999 season, said simply that his team's pitching was "just tired out and beat up" by the time Game 7 came up.

"Joe has a little flair for the dramatic. Mitch did a lot for us all year," Fregosi said. "He did a heckuva job. After he gave up the home run, he said, 'Hey, it's my fault. I didn't get the job done.' He was a stand-up guy. It's still a game. Some people have never been in that situation. Failure is a part of competition. If there is no failure, there is no game. Joe Carter has struck out with the bases loaded before. If you've never tasted failure, how good is success?"

So very true, Jim. Now, how about quirky Philly reliever Larry Andersen, a philosopher, a humorist, a jokester, who wondered, for example, why you could park in the driveway but not on the parkway.

"That series definitely could have gone either way," Andersen said. "We had our chances to win it. To their credit, when we had them down a couple of times, they came back, especially in that 15-14 game. That was a big turning point.

"One thing that really hurt us was the weather on the turf at

Joe Carter was used on billboard ads the following season.

Philadelphia. There was one ball that Lenny Dykstra could have caught had it not been wet. I think that he was a little tentative to come in on a base hit to centre. If the turf isn't wet, he's not leery of the ball skipping by. I think he laid back on the ball for what would have been the third out. That ended up costing us.

"It was a true American League game—just offence. I think the whole series was exciting. How many people can say you were in the series? Even if you lose, you get to the dance. Sometimes, you don't get asked to dance but you at least you get there. It was the thrill of my life. We were underdogs all year. Nobody expected us to do anything. I've never been on a team that played the game the way it's supposed to be played. I can't see a team like that put together again, not in talent. We had 25 characters who went out and played hard and they were unselfish."

Strange as it might sound, Andersen thought it was neat to see Carter rounding the bases and the Blue Jays whooping it up.

"It was as good to see them as it was bad to see Mitch coming off the mound and knowing he's going to be, oh, looked upon as the goat. But it wasn't all Mitch," Andersen said. "There were a lot of other things that happened. Myself in the eighth inning, I hit Tony Fernandez and he hit a grounder to first. They called it a foul ball. They said it hit off his foot. We never got to look at the ball. They threw it out. That's an out there.

31

"I ended up hitting Tony and walking Sprague to load the bases. If I don't hit Tony and I don't walk Sprague ... then Mitch comes in for the ninth, facing the eighth and ninth hitters instead of the top of the order. People want to look at Mitch as a goat. I think that's unfair. He made the season exciting. He was Mitch. A lot of people in Philadelphia wanted to get on him but the game was always interesting when he came in, whether he had a three-run lead or a one-run lead. He made it close. He had people on the edge of their seats. That's one of the things that made him so exciting. He saved 43 games. The bottom line is that he got the job done. It wasn't always pretty but he got the job done."

Phillies pitcher Curt Schilling, on many occasions, would put a white towel over her head because he couldn't stand Williams being so wild. He mocked The Wild Thing. It was a scene that didn't go over too kindly with his teammates.

"There were a few guys who wanted to go and rip that towel off his head. Yeah," Andersen said. "Him and Mitch didn't see eye to eye. To me, when you do that (what Schilling did), you're showing your teammate up. I don't think he did it originally to show Mitch up. It happened and then he got some attention from it so then he started doing it all the time. Maybe he didn't really want to watch but to do that when everyone is watching, that bothered Mitch and it bothered a lot of guys."

For Andersen's part, he was thrilled to be in the World Series, saying that "I always thought I was a mediocre pitcher in the twilight of my career but I got 15 years out of it. I have no regrets. This game's been great to me. That was the one thing about that '93 team ... I ended up playing in '94 but if I hadn't played after '93, it would've been fine but it culminated my career. It was everything .. the dream that I always thought baseball was came to fruition in '93 ... from before the game until after the game ... having a couple of beers in the clubhouse, talking about baseball, the camaraderie, it was thoughts you have as a little kid .. this is what it's like. It really wasn't always that way but in '93, very rarely was it that way the whole year. It was almost like the dream fulfilled. Anything after that was just a bonus."

Initially, when Incaviglia read the ball off Carter's bat, he made one step to the right and thought he was going to be at the wall. Then, he took another step and the ball was gone.

"It was a pretty-well-hit pitch," Incavigliaa said. "He hit it pretty good. It was down and in, off the plate. Joe put a good swing on it. I think that's what was misconstrued about that whole deal is that people (media included) blame Mitch for giving up the home run. We would never have been where we were without Mitch and his 43 saves and the job he did in the playoffs. It's too bad that a guy has to be judged by one pitch, one game.

"The whole team and the organization was behind Mitch. We didn't blame Mitch at all. We had nothing to be ashamed of. I don't think people gave Joe enough credit for the pitch that he hit. The ball wasn't down the middle of the place. It was down and in and off the plate. It was a great home run. Not a lot of people can say they won the World Series with one swing of the bat. I'm sure it's something Joe's really proud of."

Williams played that final game under death threats from fans, who had called the Phillies' office. The threats had started to come in after Game 4 of the series which the Jays won 15-14 following a fairy-tale comeback in the rain. Williams was unimpressive in that game and some Philly fans were outraged.

"If they want to come to my house, fine, but nobody is going to scare me into hiding," Williams said after Game 4.

Prior to the fifth game in Philly, there was another little melodrama that left Carter steaming mad. Stu Bykofsky, a gossip columnist with the Philadelphia Daily News, wrote that Carter and a couple of his teammates made an appearance earlier in the series at a Philly strip joint called Delilah's Den. Carter, who reputation is squeaky-clean, made it known that he was out with his family at the time he was supposed to be watching the ladies shed their clothes. At a news conference prior to Game 5, Carter seethed at the gossiper: "Where is this guy? Is he here? Ridiculous, just ridiculous."

That compared a lot to the brouhaha created the day after Game 2 by another Philadelphia Daily News columnist, Bill Conlin, who manufactured a tirade about obese Canadian singer Rita MacNeil.

MacNeil sang Canada's national anthem prior to Game 2, while Michael Bolton sang the American national anthem. The following day, the manure hit the fan when Conlin's column was revealed to Canadian onlookers.

"Towns that need a forklift," Conlin wrote, "to transport their O Canada singer to home plate should think twice before describing the Philadelphia Phillies as "unfit."

"Caution, wide-load model," Conlin added, referring to MacNeil. Conlin wondered if MacNeil was paid "by the pound, by the note, or with Jenny Craig certificates."

MacNeil, in her book, On a Personal Note, had this to say, "It was some of the most mean-spirited reporting I'd ever seen in my life, if it can be called reporting. He didn't retract his statements, nor did the Philadelphia Daily News offer an apology. In fact, he pointed out that he'd done it in the spirit of fun and that Canadians were too thin-skinned."

Later, when she was asked if she would sing for another game in the World Series, MacNeil responded by saying, "Yes, I'd do it, but only if they drive me out on the field in a forklift."

The Phillies won the fifth game to cut the Jays' series lead to 3-2, setting the stage for next game at the SkyDome. The Blue Jays took a 5-0 lead but the Phillies fought back to take a 6-5 lead in the seventh, thanks to Dykstra's three-run homer, the little man's fourth dinger of the series.

Tom Cheek, who hasn't missed a game as the Blue Jays' play-by-play man since their inception in 1977, would not say his call of Carter's homer was the most exciting of his career.

"Oh, no, no, no, I mean that would have to be the crowning moment in Joe's career, the crowning moment for Blue Jays' fans," Cheek said. "It wasn't the game winner of the first World Series in 1992 but it was a setting on Canadian soil. The country stood still in suspended animation, I suppose, for the time it took that ball to clear the fence.

"From a personal point of view, it was one of the many highlights my tenure in Toronto has provided. I suppose it would rank up there as one of the most exciting. I see milestones ... the first day in April, 1977, when I realized a dream; then there was watching George Bell sink to his knees with the final out in the game against the Yankees in 1985 for their first title of any kind; watching Dave Stieb f-i-n-a-l-l-y getting his no-hitter; a great week of baseball between the Blue Jays and Tigers in the final week in 1987.

"Joe had swung at one pitch already, a slider low and outside. He went down and got this one. That was Joe. That was Hollywood. You couldn't have written a better script. People have asked me about the call I made on it. They asked me, 'Was that planned?' How do you plan it? I'm praying for a tie game, never dreaming of a three-run homer to end it that way."

Only one other World Series ended that way. On Oct. 13, 1960, Bill Mazeroski, a good-fielding, average-hitting second baseman with the Pittsburgh Pirates, launched a Ralph Terry offering into the woods at Schenley Park beyond the left-field fence at Forbes Field to break a 9-9 tie and give the Bucs a 10-9 win over the Yankees.

"Joe should be proud because he's the first player to end a World Series with his team behind. Nobody else can say that," said Gene Tenace, who starred in several World Series with Oakland. "Guys dream of trying to get into that situation. There have been so many great players over the years but Joe is the only one in that situation."

Chapter 3

The shot heard 'round the world

Close to 50 years later, The Shot Heard 'Round The World at the Polo Grounds in New York is still remembered by some as the most famous home run ever belted in major-league history. It still echoes.

On October 3, 1951, Bobby Thomson of the New York Giants tagged a pitch by Brooklyn Dodgers' hurler Ralph Branca over the left-field fence in a special playoff game to decide the National League pennant.

The three-run shot in the bottom of the ninth inning gave the Giants a 5-4 victory and resulted in that legendary Brooklyn fan's lament: "We Wuz Robbed." It may well have been the worst day in Brooklyn's history as a borough.

Just recently, the occasion prompted the United States Postal Service to issue a special stamp. That's how legendary the home run is.

But after all these years, neither Thomson nor Branca are that interested in going out of their way to talk about it. Thomson couldn't be reached for comment after I wrote him a letter addressed to his residence in suburban New Jersey.

Branca surprisingly returned a phone call from me, forgetting I had sent a letter to his house at the Westchester Country Club in New York. After writing the letter, I called the club and was put through to his residence where his wife answered the phone and took a message.

Branca was still gracious to talk after finding out I was a reporter but made it quite clear that he has grown weary of the negativism involving his role in the home run.

"I'm tired of what's been written, tired of all the nonsense,"

Branca told me. "That's why I'm reluctant to give interviews. I'm misquoted so often. The media dwells on the negative. In the last 10 interviews I've given, eight have come up negative."

Branca says the media can't get enough of him and others in the limelight. He says one reporter based in the U.S. mid-west called him recently and said, "I'm coming to New York soon and I was wondering if you could interview you." Branca said no.

"The media slam-dunks anybody who is up high," Branca said. "Once the public gets you so high, the media wants to knock you down. I was brought into the game because I was the best pitcher on the team but people don't want to hear that."

Branca, yes, had entered the game with the score 4-2 for Brooklyn with men on second and third and a fellow by the name of Willie Mays on deck. Entering the inning, the Dodgers were leading 4-1 but the Giants chased Dodgers' pitcher Don Newcombe when Alvin Dark singled, Don Mueller singled and Whitey Lockman doubled in a run to make it 4-2.

After throwing a strike to the lean Scot from Staten Island, Branca threw a ball but Thomson, who had homered off Branca in Game 1 of the series, hit it just over the left-field fence to give the Giants the best-of-three series 2-1. New York had won the opener 3-1 and Brooklyn won 10-0 in Game 2 behind Clem Labine.

Branca said he decided on his own that he wouldn't walk Thomson intentionally and pitch to Mays, who had yet to achieve any stardom.

"The ball was high and inside. It wasn't a good pitch, the kind of pitch he had been getting me out on all season," Thomson told reporters after the game. "What a finish. Imagine being lucky enough to win a ball game that way. I had to do something.

"I had pretty much messed up things earlier. I don't imagine I looked too good running wild on the bases. After Whitey had singled, I really pulled a rock (boner) that time. I was to blame on that one. But maybe the homer made up for it.

"I know it gave me the thrill of of my life. I don't ever expect to hit another one like it."

Tied by history, Branca and Thomson, both in their 70s, are very good friends and go golfing infrequently since they live close to each other.

"Bobby and I talk a lot," Branca told me. "He's a very humble, decent human being."

"Bobby was a very classy guy," Lockman told me. "I roomed with him for a while and we played together for a long time. I was on second when he hit the homer. It was just a wild, wild dream come true.

"He had absolutely murdered the Dodgers during the last half of that season. And then he hit the home run to win the first game of the playoff. So we were all kind of surprised that they elected to pitch to him with a base open.

"The guy on deck was Willie Mays but at that point, he was a rookie and not the terror at the plate he became later. I was kind of glad they pitched to Bobby. Branca came into the game because it was Branca who gave up the home run to Bobby in the first game. It was just an incredible feeling when he hit the ball. I had some doubt at first that it would go all the way. When it did, it was just pandemonium at home plate."

Lockman, of course, tried the old, carrying-the-hero-off-the-field-on-the-shoulders trick. No such luck.

"In the old days at the old Polo Grounds, Danny, they allowed the fans to exit the park out of the stands onto the field and through a gate in centre field," Lockman told me. "By the time, I got him halfway up on my shoulders, about a thousand people had joined the mob scene and jumped up on top of him. I sprained my neck.

"I played the whole '51 World Series with a wrenched neck but it was worth it. When I got home to Dobbs Ferry, a little town just upstate from New york in Westchester County, about 250 people were in my front yard, including the mayor of the town. They proceeded to congratulate me and we had a good time."

Not only does Thomson's home run remain one of the game's most memorable but the story behind the play-by-play of the game is very intriguing.

It is with much regret that fabled and legendary announcer Ernie Harwell doesn't have a safe-keep of his call of Thomson's home run which he did while in the employ of NBC-TV, a network fashioning the first, coast-to-coast broadcast of any baseball playoff series. We'll let Harwell explain the story.

"It was a plum assignment for me. It was the first game on television across the nation," Harwell told the author. "I did the first three innings on television, Russ Hodges (Dodgers' radio sidekick) did the next three and I did the last three. There were five broadcast companies doing the game: the Dodgers, Giants,

Liberty, Mutual and Harry Caray did it for KMOX Radio in St. Louis. He had no booth so we found room for him in our booth. I was the only guy doing TV (when Thomson connected)."

Alas, in the days following the historic event, Harwell and the people at NBC couldn't find a tape of the game. They searched high and low but no luck.

"They kept no video and no audio from the television broadcast," Harwell lamented in an interview in late 1999. "They didn't tape it. It was pretty primitive. There were no replays in those days."

Fortunately, a radio tape of the home-run call was salvaged but it was a fan at the game who taped the game and sold it to Hodges for the princely sum of $10. Apparently, the fan turned on his tape recorder just in time for the historic inning and home run.

"The Chesterfield cigarette company got a hold of the tape and turned it into a promotional record and it turned out to be one of the most famous broadcasts of all time," Harwell said.

Despite being left without a tape of his own call, Harwell said it's his most memorable of all the games he's done since he began as the voice of the minor-league Atlanta Crackers out of the Marines in 1946.

"From the set point of being on the air, that was my biggest moment because it was such a big moment in baseball history," Harwell said. "The first thing I said was, 'It's gone.' But there was a moment of consternation because outfielder Andy Pasko was going up against the wall. I said to myself, 'What if he catches the ball?' But the ball ended up in the lower part of the seats over the fence. The crowd started roaring and I didn't say a word for 50 seconds."

The camera eventually found Harwell in the booth as he did his wrap on the game.

"My wife told me I had a dazed look just like the day we were married and like the day we had our kids," Harwell said.

Wonderful anecdotes from a wonderful announcer, who still calls a wonderful game in his early 80s for the Detroit Tigers and CBS Radio.

Harwell joined Brooklyn from Atlanta but not after an argument ensued between the Crackers and Dodgers.

"You can't take my guy," a Crackers' official protested. So the teams settled the dispute this way: Harwell was traded to Brooklyn in exchange for an obscure catcher. We're not making this up. It's true.

Chapter 4

Maz goes deep to stun Yankees

Bill Mazeroski has been left out in the cold too long.

Sure, he may be best known for a famous home run but he did more than just that in a span of 17 seasons in the majors. It's high time the veterans' committee responsible for electing people to the Hall of Fame looked long and hard at Mazeroski because he did more than just contribute at the plate. He was a defensive wizard around second base. Just a magician.

Voters are so much in love with hitting or pitching statistics that they tend to ignore wonderful players such as Mazeroski, who combined a reasonably solid career on offence with a ferocious appetite for splendid play around the keystone with the Pittsburgh Pirates.

Just think: Mazeroski still holds the all-time, major-league record for most double plays (1,706) in a career by a second baseman and most double plays (166 in 1966) in one season by a second sacker. After all these years, those records have been untouched. He retired after the 1972 season so for close to 30 years, he's been tops around second. He's the best the Bucs have ever had around that base, no question.

"The Hall of Fame shouldn't just be for hitting," Mazeroski told the author in late 1999. "Why can't there be someone in there for defence? It's not just a hitters' hall of fame. I played 17 years in the majors."

Mazeroski finished with a career average of .260, hit 138 homers and drove in 853 runs. On top of those double plays, he concluded his career with 4,976 putouts and 6,694 assists.

Mazeroski said no one in particular tutored him on the fine art of turning the double play. In the days when he played, there

Bill Mazeroski is Pittsburgh's all-time best second baseman.

were no specialty coaches so he fashioned the trick through what he called "trial and error."

"I backed up Maz for 10 years and not one ball went past him or under him," right-fielder Bill Virdon said in an interview. "He never made a miscue like that."

The errors he did make he kept the ball in front of him. But it's true that Maz is known basically for one feat and that was the solo home run that helped the Pirates stun the heavily favoured New York Yankees 10-9 in a wild and wooly Game 7 of the 1960 World Series on October 13.

During the regular season, the Yankees were 97-57, while the Pirates weren't far behind at 95-59. Yet, the Yankees, from the big city, were considered the Goliaths in this battle against the Davids from a much smaller city.

"Before the series began, we didn't have a chance. We weren't even supposed to get to a seventh game," Mazeroski said. "We were underdogs. That's what made it so great. We won the first game 6-4 so we thought we could play with those guys."

Mazeroski's two-run homer in Game 1 helped Pittsburgh win but the Yankees came roaring back to shellack the Bucs 16-3 behind Mickey Mantle's two homers in Game 2.

"Every game they won, they beat us by 10 runs or more," Mazeroski said. "They beat us 16-3, 10-0 and 12-0."

Whitey Ford pitched both of the shutouts but sandwiched around those romps, the Pirates also won two other games, 3-2 and 5-2, in the first six played. Game 7 was about as entertaining as you could get.

"We came back, they came back, we came back, they came back," Mazeroski said.

Leading up to the ninth inning, the most memorable moment of the game came in the eighth inning when Virdon laced a shot at shortstop Tony Kubek. Double play was written all over the ball because it was hit so hard but lo and behold, the ball hit a stone and struck Kubek in the throat.

"Bobby Chance, a left-hander, tried to hang a curve and I hit it on the nose but I said, 'Oh, no, it's a double play,' " Virdon said.

Kubek lay on the ground for a few minutes and had to be transported to hospital. The Pirates took advantage of the scenario to score five runs and take a 9-7 lead with the help of Pat Smith's two run homer.

Not to be outdone, the Yankees came back with two in the top of the ninth to tie the game 9-9.

"I was a Cleveland Indians' fan all my life and the Yankees always found ways to beat them," Mazeroski said. "And I thought they would find a way to beat us in that game. We went ahead 9-7 and I said to myself that all we had to do was go out and get three outs and we'd be winners but they came back.

"When I came back to the dugout, I was a little down because they had tied it up and someone said, 'You're up first.' I didn't know I was up first."

With Ralph Terry, the fifth New York pitcher on the hill, Mazeroski stepped in and took a high fastball. Almost immediately, Maz remembered Yankees' catcher Johnny Blanchard jumping out in front of home plate and yelling at Terry, "Keep the ball down."

On the second pitch, Terry kept the ball down a little but it was a fastball down about the letters ("lower collarbone," according to the hitter) and Mazeroski jumped on it and drilled it deep to left field where the sign said 406 feet. It took quite a poke to get it out of Forbes Field so it was awhile before it was determined what the extent of his blast was. Into Schenley Park beyond Forbes Field the ball went.

"I was always a fastball hitter," Mazeroski said. "Terry said it was a slider but it didn't slide. I hit it pretty good. I knew Yogi Berra wasn't going to catch it in left, that it would be at least off the wall. I figured it would be good for a triple and we'd have a few ways to get the run in. It was a long and high ball so it took awhile to see what was going to happen.

"But when I headed into second, the umpire signalled that it was a home run and the crowd was going crazy. When I hit third, that's when the fans started to run on the field but I made it home okay."

After the game, there was bedlam on the field and in the clubhouse. End over end, Mazeroski was patted and mobbed by his teammates and asked time and again by the media about his blast.

"It was a fan's game," Virdon said. "Everything happened ... home runs, base hits, stolen bases. It was as exciting as you'd want it to be. Nobody gave us a chance to win that series. They said it would be over in four games. You couldn't pick a better guy than Maz to achieve the feat he accomplished."

When the madness died down, Mazeroski and his wife sought solitude rather than just continue partying. So what should the couple do but walk over to nearby Schenley Park for a 90-minute breather. That's right. Not far from where his home-run ball landed, the couple had peace to themselves.

"There was no one there but us and the squirrels," Mazeroski said. "We just sat there. It was a time to relax and get away from all the excitement. After that, we went home for awhile and went downtown for some partying. The city went crazy. The city hadn't won a major championship in football (Steelers), hockey (minor-league Hornets) or baseball for about 30 years."

Chapter 5

Bucky puts a Dent in the Red Sox

"How many times have you been asked about that home run?" I asked Bucky Dent.

"Boy, if it isn't once a day. it's pretty close," he told me. "During the baseball season, you travel and people are always talking about that series and that home run."

Yes, Dent's home run off the fabled Green Monster at Fenway Park on October 1, 1978 is one of the most celebrated home runs in baseball history. It sparked the New York Yankees to a stunning 5-4 over the Boston Red Sox in a special playoff game to decide the American League East title.

A fastball in the middle and down, a 1-1 pitch he drilled into the net of the Monster.

It's an event—he hit it off Mike Torrez—Dent never gets tired of talking about. When people bring it up, it remains a good feeling.

"Yeah, it means people still remember that game, that year, that we came back from far behind," Dent said. "It means there's an awful lot of people involved that year watching that game. It was a big game, a great moment. Absolutely, the biggest moment of my career. As far as athletes think, sports is moments. As a kid growing up, you always look ... in the backyard, you talk about hitting a big home run. That was a big moment as far as my career. As far as hitting a big home run, that was it."

The Yankees were trailing 2-0 in the seventh and Dent went up to bat and almost immediately, he fouled a ball off one of his feet. He recalled having a blood clot in that foot the previous spring. Numerous times, he'd hit balls off the ankle, the blood would always go down to the leg and it would swell up. So he usually always made it a policy to wear a foam-pad leg guard. In fact, he was one of the first players to wear it that year.

"I didn't wear my guard that day," Dent confessed. "One game, I wasn't going to worry about it. I fouled a ball off my foot. I went back to the on-deck circle and they came out and put some spray on it. (Teammate) Mickey Rivers came up to me. We'd only taken a couple bats because it was only a one-day playoff. I was using one of his bats.

"I had a hairline fracture, just under the tape. He came up to me and said: 'Hey, homie, (because he's from Florida like I am) you're using the wrong bat. That one's cracked. Here, take this one. I was in so much pain. I was just ready to grab the bat. I went back in for the next pitch."

You know what happened, huh? A three-run homer.

"People always ask me, 'Did you see it go in (the screen)? And I say, no? Because at the time, we had runners on first and second, and I hit it kind of like on a line and I didn't know if it was going to get up or off the wall so I started to run real hard because I wanted to at least make a double. I didn't know until I rounded first base and saw the umpire at second base signalling that it was a home run. There's kind of like a shadow on the wall right where I hit it. I don't know who the umpire was.

"I remember coming around third base and coming home and Fenway Park was like dead silent. It was kind of like a weird feeling. It was quiet. All of a sudden, as I got more toward the dugout, you could hear the crowd start to buzz a bit, like they were in total s-h-o-c-k (Dent started to laugh here)."

The year before, Dent and Torrez had been teammates. In fact, Torrez pitched Game 6 which won the World Series for the Yankees.

"I talk to him all the time about the home run," Dent said. "He said from the time I went back to the on-deck circle, he stood on the mound and didn't throw a pitch. He like kinda lost his concentration. He didn't throw any warmups.

"And I hit the first pitch he threw when I got back in the box. He had waited five, six minutes so the first pitch he threw was the one I hit for a home run. He was pitching a great game until that moment. He said he just kinda relaxed and lost his concentration. He'd been trying to get the ball up and in on me all day. He got that pitch down and I hit it on a line. Everytime I see him, he jokes around about it.

"I wasn't a home-run hitter. I was just trying to hit the ball hard some place. Chris Chambliss and Roy White hit singles, somebody else flied out. I just happened to get it up."

Just think: Dent didn't stop his heroics there, he helped the Yankees win the AL championship over the Kansas City Royals and then proceeded to win the most-valuable player award in the World Series.

That was the year the Red Sox blew a lead of 14 and a half games to the Yankees, who ran into a lot of injuries at the start of the season and Boston was playing like .750.

"All of a sudden, they started getting hurt and we started getting guys back. Our goal was to try and make up one game per week," Dent said. "We got down to about four games and we went to Boston in September for a four-game series. They called it the Boston Nassacre because we swept them in all four. We came back home the next week and beat them 2-out-of-3. Then it came down to the last week and Boston had won seven in a row. We went to the last game and lost against the Indians."

Dent's homer against the Bosox didn't end the game and its conclusion was just as memorable for Dent as the dinger.

Carl Yastrzemski was the final hitter and Goose Gossage was the pitcher, trying to nail down the save. Gossage threw a fastball and Yastrzemski popped it up down the third-base line. Dent is standing around and sees the ball go up and all of a sudden, he feels something in his arm.

"It was like a bug in my shirt," Dent said. "I looked down and my St. Christopher medal had broken and the chain came out of my shirt. As I'm watching the ball, I'm pulling the chain out. Everybody was jumping up and down because we'd won and I'm looking for my medal. We all ran into the clubhouse and I came back out to try and find it but I couldn't. It had fallen down in my pants.

"Hitting the home run and going on to win the MVP award was tremendous. Down in Delray Beach (Florida) where I have my baseball school, we built a miniature Fenway Park with the wall and stuff like that. I kept the lineup and (announcer) Keith Jackson signed the official card he kept during the game. Every now and then, I watch the game. The tradition and the history of the Red Sox and the Yankees ... back in the 1970s, that rivalry was really intense. It was a strong division, especially the rivalry between those two teams."

Chambliss, who was on second base when Dent hit the homer said he and many others "didn't expect Bucky to hit the home run but I guess in Boston, anyone hitting right-handed has a chance to hit a home run. Bucky had power. It looked like a hanging slider to me. He said it was a fastball but it was right down the middle. During those years, we had a lot of big games like that. That one was crucial. I would say, if there was a Top 5 game I've been in, that's gotta be one of them."

Back in 1976 in Kansas City, Chambliss had hit a dramatic home run himself for the Yankees to end the AL championship series.

"The people were out on the field so it was just a mob scene so it was impossible to get to home plate," Chambliss said. "The game went back and forth. It was the same kind of drama, it had the whole season riding on it, just like the game in Boston.

"The home in Kansas City was my biggest individual moment, yes. I didn't have to touch the bases. It was not an issue at that point. Once, whenever that many people are on the field, you know, touching the bases, that's impossible. Home plate was stolen. All the bases were stolen. It was, like I said, a mob scene. Touching the bases wasn't important at that time."

For Boston manager Don Zimmer, the memories aren't good but 20 years afterward, he talked about it in a sort of non-negative fashion.

"The thing that I remember as much as anything is that at that time of the year it's usually chilly and the wind'be blowing in a little at Fenway Park, like it does at Wrigley Field when it gets cold," Zimmer said. "It was a beautiful day, the wind was drifting out just a little bit ... and when he hit it, my first reaction was, 'Good. It's an out.' Then, when I saw my left-fielder (Yaz) look up and turn around, then I know it's off the Green Monster. Then I say to myself, 'That ain't the worst thing in the world that can happen, off the wall.' Then, the next thing I see, it went into the net (for a home run).'

"The moment was tough but I thought we'd still win the game. But we didn't and ... it's a home run you don't forget. We had that big lead and we lost. Everybody said the Red Sox choked and this and that ... and I hate to even use that word. I think it's a word that stinks in our game. But that's what they were saying and writing. People don't realize it, you know, our club played like hell. I mean, we were, like, with several games to go, were one game behind the Yankees. We end up winning 99 games. The Yankees finally get beat on the last day by Rick Waits to make it a tie. I mean, I couldn't have been more prouder after we we blew 10 games. It doesn't take long to lose nine games in the standings.

"You go bad, the other team goes hot, and that's exactly what happened. But our club bounced back and played like hell. I mean it's a disgrace for somebody to say somebody choked when you won 99 games. We stopped hitting. I had a helluva lineup, an awesome offensive lineup, and we just went into a slump and we just couldn't score. Then when we got out of it, we played like hell again."

Chapter 6

Fisk's waving-fair homer epitomized best-ever World Series

C arlton Fisk asked for divine intervention as the clock headed toward 1 a.m. on October 22, 1975 in the 12th inning. He jumped up and down, waving his hands frantically like he was trying to part the sea or stand on water.

He was granted his wish. The ball he drilled toward the left-field corner stayed fair, striking the foul-pole screen and setting off one of the most joyous occasions in New England.

The home run ended a four-hour marathon and what might be the most wonderful, entertaining game in the best-ever World Series ever played. It was dynamite theatre.

Fisk's career legacies are longevity, an ability to skillfully call a game behind the plate and being a pretty decent offensive player, who hit 376 home runs.

He'll be remembered, too, for his dramatic departure from the Red Sox a few years later after the team sent him a contract too late, a miscue noted by Fisk's wife, Janet, who saw the postage stamp bore a date of Dec. 21, 1979, one day following the deadline for tendering contracts.

It is speculated that Boston general manager Haywood Sullivan deliberately sent the contract late. Fisk signed with the White Sox and he remained with them until being cut in 1993 after he set the major-league record for most games caught by a receiver.

He'll also be remembered for shouting at Deion (Prime Time) Sanders, the two-sport star, when the latter diddled around home plate after grounding out. "Run the @*$#+ ball out," Fisk screamed at the New York Yankees' player. Fisk couldn't stand mediocrity and maybe Sanders got the message.

But Fisk's home run is the event he will be remembered most for, the defining moment of his career, even though the Red Sox didn't win the World Series. The Cincinnati Reds captured Game 7 with a 4-3 win on Joe Morgan's bloop-single RBI in the 10th inning. Fisk's homer had given the Red Sox a 7-6 win and forced a seventh and deciding game.

Luis Tiant, the bearded, paunchy, Cuban-born pitcher, got the Red Sox off on the right foot in the first game with a complete-game 6-0 win, his fifth consecutive at Fenway. It sure helped that Tiant's parents were in the stands after they travelled from Cuba. Seven weeks earlier, Tiant had embraced his parents for the first time in 15 years.

"He pitching well," Luis Sr. told the media not long after Game 1 concluded.

"He's telling me what I've been doing wrong," Luis Jr. said about his father. "He says I'm making mistakes on some guys. He says I should be using my head when I'm on the mound."

Ten Boston batters took their turn at the plate in the seventh inning and the Red Sox scored all their runs, two of them on a base hit by Rico Petrocelli. The barrage of runs was triggered by a throwing error by Reds pitcher Don Gullett. He had fielded a bunt by Dwight Evans and threw the ball past second base trying to get the forceout.

"The key to the whole game was Tiant," Boston manager Darrell Johnson told reporters after the game.

"Tiant put zeroes on the scoreboard all game long," added Cincinnati skipper Sparky Anderson. "And I don't know how much better you can be than that. But I'll give you a little advice—everybody stay calm because I am."

Sparky, of course, was telling people not to get too excited about the Reds losing. During the regular season, the "mean, red machine" had won 108 games and lost only 54, while the Red Sox were 95-65. So the Reds were favoured to win the World Series. In the playoffs, the Reds topped the Pittsburgh Pirates and the Beantowners disposed of Oakland.

Game 2 of the '75 World Series saw the Reds tie things up with a 3-2 win, thanks in part to Dave Concepcion's speed. The big Venezuelan was on first with two out in the ninth inning with the score tied 2-2. With 33 stolen bases during the regular season, he was a threat to move another 90 feet.

In a controversial play at second, Concepcion was ruled safe on a steal, although Boston second baseman Denny Doyle argued that he had tagged the runner before he reached the bag.

"He think he got me out but he tagged me on on the back when I'm already on the bag," Concepcion said.

Concepcion apparently missed the bag initially but noted that Doyle didn't "return for the tag". Ken Griffey Sr. came through in the clutch with a double to score Concepcion with the go-ahead run.

It was a heart-breaker for the Bosox because Bill (Spaceman) Lee had pitched brilliantly into the ninth as Boston clung to a 2-1 lead. Johnny Bench doubled off Lee to open the ninth and that prompted Johnson to bring in Dick Drago. Bench moved to third on a high-bouncing out to second by Tony Perez.

Tension mounted when Bench was forced to stay at third on George Foster's short fly to left which was stationed by strong-armed Carl Yastrzemski. But Concepcion singled home Bench with two out and the game was tied.

"We were lucky to get out of there with our lives," Anderson said after the game.

Game 3 went to the Reds 6-5 but it wasn't without another controversy that resulted in Cincinnati winning the game. Home-plate umpire Larry Barnett, a World Series rookie in his occupation, ruled that there was no interference after Fisk collided with Reds' hitter Ed Armbrister a few feet from home plate in the 10th inning.

With Cesar Geronimo on first with nobody out, Armbrister bunted and as he dallied while getting out of the batter's box, Fisk lunged for the ball but he ran into Armbrister.

Fisk grabbed the ball and threw to second to try to force Geronimo but the ball sailed into centre field. Geronimo went to third and Armbrister ended up at second.

"I ruled it was simply a collision," Barnett said after the game. "It is interference only when the batter intentionally gets in the way of the fielder."

The rule book doesn't mention the word "collision" when the batter or runner fails to avoid a fielder, who is attempting to field a batted ball. Armbrister, as replays showed, didn't avoid Fisk. Johnson, Fisk and Co. argued to no avail.

"It's a gawdamn shame to lose a gawdamn game because of the gawdamn call," said a furious Fisk, as he spit chewing tobacco on the carpet around his cubicle. Then he vented his frustration on three magazines which he grabbed and hurled across the clubhouse.

"He (Armbrister) stood there," Fisk continued. "I had to go up for a rebound over him to get the ball."

The next day, Barnett said he "slept good" and added, "If I had to do it over again, I'd do it the same way."

It was learned later in the series that Barnett received a death threat via letter against himself, his wife and small child.

The letter told Barnett to fork over $10,000 in ransom or he would get a ".38-calibre bullet in your head" if Boston loses the series. No doubt Barnett was upset by the letter.

"You have to have in the back of your mind that the person is deranged," Barnett told a reporter with the New York Times at the time. "When they shoot at the (U.S.) president twice in a month, that's what scares you."

Game 3 featured six homers, including Fisk's which gave the Boston an early 1-0 cushion. But homers by Bench, Concepcion and Geronimo gave the Reds a 5-1 lead. Back came the Red Sox— Bernie Carbo belted a pinch-hit, two-run homer to make it 5-3 and Dwight Evans stunned the crowd by tying the game with a two-run shot in the ninth.

With the score tied 5-5 in the 10th, Geronimo legged out a single behind second base off Jim Willoughby. That set the stage for Armbrister's attempted bunt.

"Our man was interfered with," Johnson said. "He (Armbrister) got in the catcher's way."

In Game 4, Boston beat Cincinnati 5-4 to tie the series 2-2 in a rather uneventful match, perhaps the most uneventful of the series. The contest was settled in the fourth inning on Yastrzemski's go-ahead RBI single.

The Bosox scored all their runs in that inning and settled back to watch Tiant go the distance for his second complete game of the series. Tiant wheezed and puffed his portly frame to 163 pitches.

"Luis is the best I've got," Johnson said after the game. "He's a very strong man."

Tiant, who wasn't exactly a guy interested in staying in shape, brushed off comments about getting tired on so many pitches.

"I don't care if it's 3,000 pitches as long as I win," Tiant said.

In Game 5, Perez wrestled a gorilla off his back by breaking out of an 0-for-15 slump to power the Reds to a 6-2 win and give Cincy a 3-2 series lead.

Perez hit a three-run homer and a solo shot to lead the offence and Gullett fired two-hit ball over eight innings before giving way to the bullpen.

"Don Gullett dominated the ball game," Johnson said.

But so did Perez, who was relegated to fifth in the order from the clean-up spot for the game. After striking out in the first inning, Perez blasted both of his homers off Reggie Cleveland.

"This was a four-day slump," Perez said after his implosion. "If the slump had happened during the regular season, nobody would think about it."

Game 6, well, it took three days before it was played because of rainstorms that battered New England. Leading up to the first possible day the teams could play after the usual one off-day between switches in venues, Boston's off-the-wall pitcher, Bill Lee, remarked, "I don't think those guys (Reds) can hit in a rainstorm but I can pitch in one."

What finally followed when the teams did get to play the sixth game was a barnburner. To this day, Game 6 is heralded by some as perhaps the most entertaining baseball game ever played, period. Sure, there are some who may argue but the game sure ranks right up there with the best.

At some point during the game, Pete Rose of the Reds was chatting with Fisk and remarked, "Some kind of game, isn't it?"

Fisk replied, "Some kind of game.I don't think anyone could ask for a better game than this."

Not remembered by many people is that Fisk made two, stupendous defensive plays in the top of the 12th before he traded his mitt for the bat in the bottom half of the inning. First, Fisk made a great lung to grab a pop-up by Bench, and then he threw to second to force Rose on a sac-bunt attempt by Griffey.

"I never swing for a home run," Fisk said after the home run which resulted in many Boston fans storming the field to congratulate him.

"Even if I had to straight-arm people or knock them down, I made sure I touched every bit of white out there," Fisk said later.

Out in the vicinity of the third-base coach's box, Red Sox coach Don Zimmer was motioning for divine intervention as Fisk's blast sailed past him.

"I'm on the line doing the same thing as Fisk, trying to wave the ball fair," Zimmer told the author years later. "Fisk is waving his arms trying to get the ball fair and I'm doing the same thing but you can't see me.

"You see, at Fenway, you have to jump out on the line to even see the foul line. I mean ... that home run ... I'll never forget."

Bet you don't know who gave up that home run, eh? A good trivia question. Let the drums bang slowly. A guy by the name of Pat Darcy, that's who. He was out of the game by 1976 but in '75, he compiled an 11-5 record with 22 of his 27 appearances being starts. In '76, he appeared in only 11 games and never appeared in the majors again.

The only reason the game went into extra innings was traced to a fellow by the name of Carbo. He provided awesome theatrics with a 400-foot, three-run homer off Rawly Eastwick in the fifth inning, for his second homer in as many games, to knot the game at 6-6. It was his second pinch-hit homer of the series.

"Bernie Carbo, talking about home runs ... he took two, very meek swings and then on the next pitch, he hit it over the centre-field fence," Zimmer said.

"It was a fastball over the plate," Carbo told reporters at the time. "I was telling myself not to strike out and with four days off between games, I was just trying to put the ball in play somewhere."

In the ninth, the Red Sox had a chance to end the game by loading the bases but they couldn't get a run in.

In the 11th inning, Evans had made a sensational catch off Morgan near the right-field seats to start a double play, a highlight-reel scenario in itself.

"It was probably as good a ball game as I've ever seen," Anderson said at the time. "That catcher by Evans was as good as you'll ever see."

Game 7 didn't quite live up to the magic spun by Game 6 but the game went into extra innings just the same. This was a game the Red Sox seemed to have sewn up because they led 3-0 as late as the sixth inning. The curse of the Bambino seemed to be over ... the Red Sox appeared on the verge of winning their first World Series since 1918.

Perez slammed a two-run homer — off a lob ball thrown by Lee — to stun the Red Sox and bring the Reds within a run at 3-2. Then Rose delivered an RBI single off Lee in the seventh and the score was tied 3-3. Within minutes, Lee was out of the game because of a blister on his throwing thumb.

Then in the bottom of the ninth, the moment of truth arrived. During the regular season, the Reds had won 26 games in their last at-bat. A non-household name answering to Jim Burton will go down in the record books as the losing pitcher in the best-ever World Series.

Griffey drew a walk and Geronimo picked him up by executing a sacrifice bunt. With two out following a groundout, Griffey was at third and Rose was at the plate. Burton pitched very carefully to Rose and finally, he drew a base on balls.

So with men on the corners, Joe Morgan came to the plate. Morgan broke all the suspense and ended the series by swinging at a ball away from the heart of the plate and flaring a 200-foot single to centre, just in front of Fred Lynn, who had no play at the plate. Game over. Series over. The Reds won both the game and the series 4-3. It was Cincinnati's first World Series win since 1940.

"The pitch Morgan hit was a very good pitch," Burton said. "It was a slider low and away. I'm not going around beating my head about it. It's not like I killed a person."

Over in the Reds' clubhouse, Anderson called the series "the greatest" ever played. We're the best team in baseball but not by much."

Said Rose, "I thought the sixth game was the best ever played but I've got to change that. This game was the best ever."

Twenty-five years later, Fisk and Perez were laughing and smiling about the wonderful series and Fisk's homer in Game 6 as they chatted with reporters regarding their Jan. 11, 2000 selection to the Hall of Fame.

"I was trying to wave the ball foul and Carlton was trying to wave it fair," Perez said.

Scores in '75 Series			
Boston	6	Cincinnati	0
Cincinnati	3	Boston	2
Cincinnati	6	Boston	5 (10 innings)
Boston	5	Cincinnati	4
Cincinnati	6	Boston	2
Boston	7	Cincinnati	6 (12 innings)
Cincinnati	4	Boston	3

Chapter 7

Henderson's homer dooms Moore

Dave Henderson's famous homer off Donnie Moore on October of 1986 didn't end the American League championship series. It didn't even end that game.

The two-run homer gave the Boston Red Sox a 6-5 lead and what some people don't realize is that the California Angels came back to tie the game before Moore gave up a sacrifice fly that gave Boston a 7-6 win in the 11th inning.

Guess who hit the sac fly? None other than Henderson, who came up with the bases loaded after Don Baylor was hit by a pitch, Dwight Evans singled and Rich Gedman legged out a bunt single that was really intended as a sacrifice to move the runners over.

That home run by Henderson, though, is still rated by many as one of the most stunning hits in the game's history. This was one time when the Angels finally appeared close to going to the World Series for the first time. Moore, taunted and haunted by the memory along with the break-up of his marriage and the end of his career, shot himself less than three years later on July 18, 1989 with a semi-automatic, .45-calibre that his wife Tonya had purchased for him.

"He loved guns," Tonya told me years later. "He hunted quail, pheasant, deer, boar."

That day, he shot humans. Just before pulling the trigger on himself, Donnie almost killed Tonya with several blasts to the chest. It did all in front of his three children at their home in the Peralta Hills, a swank, exclusive enclave located within swanky Anaheim Hills, not far from Anaheim Stadium in Orange County.

A month before shooting himself, Moore pretty much knew his career was over when the Kansas City Royals released him from employment with their Triple-A club in Omaha.

"After his release by Kansas City, I left home because there was no more baseball for him," Tonya, an abused spouse for many years, told me. "I was tired of taking all the beatings. I had it in my gut that it was going to be miserable. With one of those blows, one of these times, it was going to be fatal. The beatings had been going on since I was 18 or 19 and I wasn't going to take it anymore. He was a very nice but he was very possessive."

Tonya survived the shooting but it was miraculous that none of the shots hit her arteries. Doctors say it was amazing she didn't die. The first shot hit her in the neck and then when she tried to escape, he fired again.

"One shot was below my boobs and another shot hit me in the boobs," Tonya said. "They went through my lungs and went out my backside."

Ronnie, 8, one of the couple's sons, leaned over his father's limp body to dial 911.

"In the hospital, I saw on television that they brought Donnie's body out in a bag," Tonya said. "That's when I knew he was dead. I was in ICU. I was so drugged."

Before Donnie was buried, Tonya arranged for his body to be brought to the hospital so she could see him for one, last time. Strange, but true.

"I wanted to give my last respects," she said. "It looked like he was sleeping."

For a long time following Henderson's home run, Moore would mention Ralph Branca's name on many occasions. Branca coughed up a similar home run in the 1951 National League playoff game to Bobby Thomson. Moore's career legacy appears to be that home run, just like Bill Buckner's career legacy is booting that groundball by Mookie Wilson a week or so after Moore's faux pas. Buckner, the first baseman for Boston, gets the goat horns over one lousy grounder, even though he collected over 2,700 lifetime hits.

Moore threw Dave Henderson a forkball on that fateful pitch and admitted later that he should have continued firing fastballs at him.

"I blew it," Moore told reporters at the time. "He hit an off-speed pitch. He was fouling off fastballs. I should have stayed hard with him. I'm a human being and I didn't do the job. But I won't blame it on my sore shoulder."

Tonya Moore, Donnie's widow, knows Donnie was really wounded by that home run but by how much?

"You would have to ask Donnie about that but being with him, it affected him a lot," Tonya told me. "How he really felt, I don't know. After that, the fans booed. The minute he put his head out of the dugout before a game, they'd boo him. Reggie Jackson thrived on people booing him but Donnie couldn't do that. He'd rather be on the road.

"Those fans have no right to sit in our section, the families' section, right behind the net at home plate. Baseball players are human. They're human like everybody else. The fans were brutal. I'd like to see them get out there and see what they can do. They don't know anything.

"They think that because players make all this money that they should be perfect. That bothers me inside. Players are only human. Do you think a pitcher actually wants to see a home run or major run come home?

"My first thought after that home run was, 'How did Donnie feel?' " Tonya was saying. "He didn't look too good out there. The Angels knew he had a sore arm. Without him, the Angels would never have been there in the first place. He took all the blame for them losing the series but we had two chances to still win that game. It wasn't Donnie's fault that the Angels didn't go to the World Series. He didn't lose that game by himself. Boston still had two games to win."

That's right. The Angels, a team haunted and taunted like Moore because of all the tragedies that have beset the franchise since its inception in 1962, still led the series 3-2 despite the spell-binding loss.

Yet, when the Red Sox won the final three games, the home run took on a greater prominence. Close to 10 years later, the whole affair resulted in a book called One Pitch Away by Mike Sowell. Yes, the Angels were only one pitch away from advancing to their first World Series when Henderson took Moore downtown.

At the time of Moore's death, catcher Brian Downing of the Angels had some harsh words, not for the fans, but for the media.

"You buried the guy," Downing said. "He was never treated fairly. He wasn't given credit for all the good things he did. Nobody was sympathetic. It was always, 'He's faking it. He's fooling around.' I never, ever saw the guy be credited for getting us to the playoffs because all you ever heard about, all you ever read about was one ... pitch."

Following Moore's death, it wasn't long before Tonya moved out of the house, which she eventually sold for a loss at about the same price as the couple purchased it for, $700,000. She knew why she had to settle for a bargain-basement price with the buyer.

"Nobody wanted to live in a house where someone died," she told me. "Nobody would say that but that's exactly why. I could never stay in that house at night. After he died, I never stayed in a room with the doors closed. They were always open. I would walk down to the lake and I thought he was there. It was unreal. I would sit at the top of the stairs on the dock and I would feel him down there."

Sadly, Donnie's family in Texas holds a grudge against Tonya and her kids: Demetria, like her mom, is 5-foot-11, Donnie Jr. is 6-foot-4 and Ronnie, like his father was, is a 6-footer.

"My kids don't see Donnie's family," Tonya said. "His family totally holds me responsible, as the reason their son is dead. It's strange. How could they possibly think I was responsible?"

Tonya Moore stayed with Donnie even though he was an alcoholic, who devoured Jack Daniel's on the rocks like it was going out of style.

"Sometimes, he'd be an asshole and beat my ass but he was a very good person," Tonya said. "I loved the hell out of Donnie Moore. Donnie was a sweetheart. His death was a rude awakening. You try to deal with the pain but you live it for as long as you live. I miss my husband. He loved me very much. I know he did."

Chapter 8

60, 61, 62, 70, 66, 65, 63, 714, 755

For over 50 years since his death, baseball fans still celebrate the Babe. He just may be the most popular player to have ever graced the game as we begin work on the 21st century.

His phenomenal power, his magnetic personality, his lifestyle of womanizing, boozing, eating, his genuine, down-to-earth link with kids and fans in general when he was alive, have all contributed to the lore of the Bambino. If he had not chased women and drank like a fish, then maybe he wouldn't be so popular today.

Instead, his legend will live on for eternity. Figurines are still being churned out to celebrate George Herman Ruth's memory. Sports Illustrated, in late 1999, voted him baseball's top player of the 20th century.

At the height of his success with the Yankees in the 1920s, Ruth was the game's highest-paid player and rightly so. In 1924, he signed a two-year contract worth $52,000 a year. Later on, he earned a deal that paid him $80,000 per annum.

When all the money came pouring in, he didn't hide from the fans. He flaunted success by buying expensive convertibles and driving down the street and

Babe Ruth figurine

waving at fans, who would wave in return.

Of course, the Bambino is most legendary for his home runs. On September 19, 1927, Babe Ruth became the first player in the majors to crank out 60 home runs and it came off Tom Zachary of the Washington Senators. The record lasted until 1961 when Roger Maris, another Yankee, hit 61. Maris' mark would hold the test of time until 1998 when both Mark McGwire of the St. Louis Cardinals and Sammy Sosa of the Chicago Cubs hit 70 and 66 respectively.

In 1999, Big Mac and Slammin' Sammy did it again: McGwire with 65, Sosa with 63.

Ruth finished his career with a record 714 dingers and he would have had more, except that his first five years in the bigs were devoted almost entirely to pitching. Who's to say he wouldn't have finished with 800 homers, if he had concentrated solely on hitting. On the days he didn't head to the mound, he rarely hit. His at-bats in 1915, 1916 and 1917: 92, 136 and 123, respectively. He hit a total of nine homers.

In 1914, Ruth was called up by the Boston Red Sox in mid-season after winning 11 games for the minor-league team in

Baltimore. In 1915, he blossomed in his first full season by going 18-8 and in 1916, he was stupendous with a 23-12 record and 1.75 ERA. He just got better and better. In 1917, he won 24 games.

As World War I was nearing its end, it became clear that Ruth's potential was at the plate, not on the pitching rubber. His at-bats increased to 317 in 1918 and he responded with 11 homers and 66 RBI, while on the mound, he was 13-7 with a 2.22 ERA in 166.1 innings pitched.

Babe Ruth

By 1919, he was pitching less (9-5, 133.1 IP) and hitting more (432 AB, 29 homers, 101 RBI).

Following the 1919 season, Red Sox owner Harry Frazee needed some money to pay off some entertainment bills and in one of the worst transactions ever made, Ruth was dealt to the Yankees on Jan. 3, 1920. In exchange, Frazee received $125,000 and a $300,000 loan.

In 1920, the Yankees decided to use Ruth almost exclusively as a hitter and in only 458 AB, he ripped 54 homers and drove in 158 runs ... the Babe had only just begun his ferocious attack on opposition pitching. In 1921, he hit 59 homers, the most he would hit until 60 in 1927.

In 1922, he did experience a fall between the lines. He was suspended for the first 39 games of the season after his waistline expanded dramatically due to his notion that training was a nuisance and because he had engaged in a barnstorming tour.

Ruth had also emerged as a man with a short fuse. Further suspensions and fines followed and all in all, it was a mini nightmare of a season: 35 homers, 99 RBI in 405 at-bats.

Following that season, he got a rude awakening at a party when soon-to-be New York mayor Jimmy Walker confronted the Babe and said, "Are you going to let those kids down again?"

Ruth began to cry in front of the gathered folks and promised to ship up by getting into shape at his off-season home in Massachussetts. What does he do in 1923? .393 average, a career-high 205 hits, 41 taters and 131 RBI. He also walked a career-high 170 times. The Babe was back in form.

Ruth played with the Yankees through the 1934 season when he hit 34 homers and collected 114 RBI at age 39. The following season, he slipped to 22 homers and 84 RBI.

Between 1920 and 1933, he pitched only five times. His last appearance came against his old team, the Red Sox, and he went the distance in a 6-5 Yankees' win.

His first and last seasons were spent in Boston. 1935 saw him playing for the Braves of the National League and he came to the plate only 72 times with six dingers and 22 RBI. He finished with 714 homers, a record he held until Hank Aaron broke it close to four decades later. Aaron finished his career with 755.

For 12 years following his exit from the game, Ruth's life was almost uneventful. Then came news in 1947 that he had become gravelly ill. He was never told that he had cancer but that's what hit him. He was diagnosed with having a malignant tumour on the left side of his neck. A ligation of the arter-

Ruth in civilian clothes
(Photo, Conlin Collection,
American Historical Society)

ies that supplies the face, tongue and other parts of the head was undertaken but it did little to halt the spread of cancer to other parts of his body.

For several years, he was in out of hospitals and in great pain, although a drug called teropterin relieved some of it. On July 21, 1948, Ruth received the last rites. That's how far he had deteriorated.

Five days later with great difficulty, Ruth got out of his hospital bed in New York City to visit the Astor Theater to witness the premiere of his life, The Babe Ruth Story, starring William Bendix.

"Ruth left Memorial Hospital to see the movie, insulated by a police cordon from a pushy, cheering throng of more than 1,000," the New York Times reported. "The Bambino, who last played in the majors in 1935, walked slowly into the theater. He was supported by both arms, perspiring heavily and seemingly too ill and too tired to do anything but smile wanly and painfully at the avid crowd." Other movie goers included Notre Dame football coach Frank Leahy, Mrs. Lou Gehrig, St. Louis Cardinals manager Eddie Dyer, Joe Dugan, a Yankees' third baseman and former mate of Ruth, and Charles Comiskey, the 22-year-old owner of the White Sox.

Ruth, the mightiest hitter in the game in his era, was near death's door. A few weeks later on Aug. 16, a special bulletin was released by Memorial Hospital, saying that the Babe was "sinking rapidly."

That memo to the media was soon heard by people all around North America and it precipitated a phenomenal response of 15,000 phone calls and telexes (that's right) to the hospital from Canadians and Americans.

Two hours later and five days after being placed on the critical list, Ruth died of cancer of the throat. The Times' front-page headline the next day read:

Babe Ruth, Baseball Idol, Dies At 53 After Lingering Illness

"He said his prayers and lapsed into a sleep. He died in his sleep," said priest Rev. Thomas Kaufman. Among those with him at his bedside were the Babe's wife, Claire, and his two adopted daughters, Mrs. Daniel Sullivan and Mrs. Richard Flanders.

Unfortunately like Ruth, Maris died of cancer at roughly the same age. Maris died at age 51, less than two weeks before Christmas in 1985, a guy unadmired for his success, so much so that then commissioner Ford Frick put an asterisk beside the short-time slugger's name when he slammed 61 in '61. Why? Because Maris took more games to break the record.

McGwire in butter sculpture

The Babe played during an era when teams played 154 games, while Maris had the advantage of a 162-game schedule. But for the record, Maris actually hit his 61st in the 159th game he personally participated in on the last day of the season in the team's 162nd game. Ruth his 60th in his 151st game. McGwire's 62nd? He drilled it in only the 137th game in which he actually served duty. Remember, Big Mac missed a lot of games due to injury but still broke the record.

Frick's demand only made him look like a horse's ass and diminished Maris' run at the record. The New York media seemed to take Frick's side and the publicity convinced the general populace to believe in the commissioner's twisted logic. So, if you can believe it, less than 23,000 fans showed up at the House that Ruth Built the day Maris hit his 61st off Tracy Stallard.

"I am the luckiest hitter in baseball history," Maris said after breaking the Babe's mark. "If what I can do from now cannot count toward the official record, there's no sense in yapping."

Maris survived the heat from the media in '61 to break the Babe's mark but the homer feat will never get him into the Hall of Fame. He just wasn't a superstar over an extended period of time. He was a star, okay, for a brief period. Like he did in '61, he captured the AL's MVP award in 1960.

Unlike the Babe, Maris loathed publicity. Dealing with the media wasn't his cup of tea. He was a quiet, shy person, 27, fired

Photo by Danny Gallagher

Harvey Townsend of Toronto paid tribute to slugger Mark McGwire by manufacturing a magnificent, life-size butter sculpture weighing 150 pounds. The sculpture was on display at the 1998 Royal Winter Fair in Toronto. "It's a delicacy," said Townsend, who is 77-years-old. "I did some preliminary work of the character of the face in clay in my studio at home and did the rest of it at the fair. I knew Mark was a big man, 6-foot-5, 250 pounds. I was given photos from several newspaper and off the Internet. It's difficult to do people from a photograph. I'd rather have the person to work with." Townsend still fashioned an eerie likeness of McGwire, goatee included. "It took about a period of a month to do it," said Townsend, a native Britoner. Sad to say, the sculpture was broken up in pieces following the fair and taken by the Gay Lea dairy-food company to its plant in Geesworth, Ontario, near Toronto. There, the butter was used to help concoct an East Indian delight called gee.

into the spotlight of a glorious season in the media city of the world. The tabloids wanted him on the front or back page but he would have preferred page 37 or whatever.

Maris would have opted for a glass cage where he could have put up a sign saying, "No interviews today." Instead, Maris agreed to see the media before and after every game. Still, he was scorned. Yankees' fans wanted Mickey Mantle, cut from royalty, the career Yankee and penultimate slugger, to break the record because he had been with the team much longer than Maris, an adopted son, who joined the Bronx Bombers the previous season after stints with the Cleveland Indians and Kansas City Athletics.

The New York fans never seem to forgive Maris for shattering the Babe's mark. Even the Bronx media was mean-spirited. On the day after the Yankees swapped him to the St. Louis Cardinals during the winter of 1966-67 following his seven seasons there, one reporter was loath to say, "The Maris story is one of unfullfillment, a progression from triumph to ashes, at least partly self-inflicted."

During his record run in '61, Maris batted .269, scored

132 runs and knocked in 141. He was walked 94 times and struck out just 67 times. A wonderful season.

During McGwire's run at Maris' record in 1998, Maris got some justice and more appreciation for what he did. His image was resurrected or reborn in death. Newspaper reporters talked about Maris extensively when it became apparent that Big Mac would bear down on the record. Roger Jr. made a trip to almost every park in the majors that season in memory of his father.

McGwire started the 1998 season with a grand slam opening day and waged a battle all season with Sosa to see who would shatter 61 first. On Sept. 8 with the Maris family among the estimated 50,000 fans watching from the stands and with Sosa and the Cubs visiting Busch Stadium in St. Louis, McGwire blasted No. 62 off Steve Traschel just inside the left-field foul pole.

The fans greeted McGwire with an 11-minute standing ovation and the sea of red in St. Loo gave Sosa a similar but shorter clap.

"I'm absolutely speechless," McGwire said later. "The fans here are great and that's why I'm happy I was able to hit this homer here. I've been talking about this since January. I'm one swing away and the ball disappears on me. I really believe in fate."

At a ceremony following the home run, McGwire was presented with the ball by the "catcher" in the stands, Tim Formeris. McGwire held the ball up triumphantly.

"I wanted the Maris family to know that their father is in my heart," McGwire told the crowd. "When I held his (Maris') bat before the game, I touched it to my heart. Now, I know my bat will be next to his in the Hall of Fame and I'm damn proud of it."

The record-breaker produced a spectacular, special edition of the St. Louis Post-Dispatch the following day and it resulted in an additional $900,000 (U.S.) in additional revenue for the paper because 1.55-million copies were sold, some 1.2-million more than the traditional daily-print run of 330,000. Amazing.

McGwire didn't stop there. He finished with 70 homers but down near the end, he did have to wage another battle with Sosa because the Cubs' star didn't give up easily. He twice led McGwire in the chase after May 16, only to see Big Mac take over shortly thereafter.

Sosa slammed 66 of his own, a remarkable and incredulous total for a player, who was embarking on his first season of greatness after a number of seasons in mediocrity.

McGwire hit Nos. 69 and 70 on the final day of the season, again in St. Louis, off the Montreal Expos. Needless to say, the Cardinals' fans gave the larger-than-life slugger several standing Os. McGwire had gone into the final game with a 68-66 lead on Sosa, who was held homerless. Sosa was also homerless in the one-day playoff game against San Francisco.

Throughout the season, public support seemed to be in Sosa's favour because he appeared to be loving the spotlight, kibiting with ease with the media, while McGwire grew weary of the daily barrage of questions. At one point, he insisted on some space when he decided he would talk only before the first game of each series and then after a game in which he hit a home run.

McGwire would always criticize the media by downplaying the chase to beat Maris' mark. While he was with Oakland prior to being traded to St. Loo, McGwire was always accommodating with the media but the larger-than-life attention he got while on the home-run chase made him a testy star, who nonetheless, drew people like magnets to ballparks around the majors, as did Sosa.

"Fifty hears from now, I hope they remember me," Sosa told reporters at one point. "Mark's the man. I've been saying that all year."

But give McGwire credit, he came back in 1999 and almost matched his '98 total. Ditto for Sosa.

For the record, the all-time professional record for most homers in one season belongs to Joe Baumann, who ripped 72 homers and drove in 224 runs to go along with a .400 average in 1954 while playing for the Class C minor-league team in Roswell, New Mexico.

"The ball looked like a cantaloupe all season," Baumann once told a reporter.

For his part, Aaron doesn't get near the credit he should be getting for he did—755 homers—and neither does Willie Mays, who is third in lifetime homers with 660. Mays was voted second best baseball player in the 20th century by Associated Press after Ruth.

Aaron's 755 mark has stood the test of time since his retirement in 1976 but Ken Griffey Jr. is considered the player most likely to threaten it, possibly by 2005.

Babe Ruth died of throat cancer on Aug. 16, 1948 at age 53.
Roger Maris died of lymphatic cancer on Dec. 14, 1985 at age 51.

Chapter 9

Jackson 'straw that stirs the drink'

Bobby Winkles remembers Reggie Jackson, his centre-fielder at Arizona State University, as a terrific baseball player, who could hit for power and utilize a deadly accurate arm to hit the cut-off man all the time.

It was that deadly arm that made a splashing display during the 1974 World Series when Mr. October, then playing for Oakland, took a long hit near the fence from Bill Buckner, turned and fired a strike to second-baseman Dick Green, who in turn zipped a throw to third baseman Sal Bando, who tagged Buckner, trying to leg out a triple.

It's a story Winkles likes to share because by that time, he had reached the majors himself as Oakland's third-base coach.

Winkles also remembers the man, too, for his academic prowess at ASU.

"Reggie was a very intelligent person," said Winkles, a former, long-time baseball coach at ASU. "As a matter of fact, he carried 19 units a semester. He took a speech-classes course on the fundamentals of speech.

"Most students, it's 15 units. And he turned out a B average. He was one of the few guys to go back to college and finish school. At Arizona State, if a player didn't follow the rules, he became a student, instead of a student-athlete. If a player became a student only, it meant he was off the team."

That's how stern Winkles and the university were. Jackson was also an all-conference football player at ASU and "he was a damn-good basketball player," Winkles said.

"He had such great athletic ability. You could tell that by all those home runs he hit. He was a tremendous competitor. He always played hard, ran hard. He was a great athlete, a fine young

Photos courtesy Oakland Athletics

Reggie Jackson is in a talking mood in his early days with Oakland. Inset photo is an older Jackson with Oakland in his final season in the majors in 1987.

Reggie Jackson was known for taking mighty swings during stellar career.

man. He ran the 100-yard dash in 9.6 seconds."

When Jackson reached the majors with the Kansas City Athletics in 1967, it was the beginning of an illustrious career that would span 20 seasons. He could hit for power, he could run for a big guy and he could talk the talk.

"Reggie was a very fiery, competitive guy. He had a big ego," Ed Sprague Sr., a former Oakland teammate, told the author. "He always liked to be out front but when it came time to compete, he definitely did that. He was definitely a team player. I remember times when he'd come back to the bench after hitting a long home run and he'd say, 'How far did it go?' He'd joke

71

Reggie Jackson and Jack Howell of the Angels get ready for a 1986 game.

about it."

Jackson's trash talking once prompted another former mate, Darold Knowles, to make this provocative statement: "There isn't enough mustard in this world to cover that hot dog."

Knowles said it's true he made the statement in 1971 or 1972 but that it never made headlines until spring training in 1978 when he was playing for Texas and Jackson was heading into his second season with the New York Yankees.

"Ron Bergman, a writer with the Oakland Tribune, got the quote and kept it and didn't come out with it until later," Knowles told me. "And when it came out, he tried to create a feud between me and Reggie. It came out nationally and in some magazines. Reggie and I laughed about it. I wasn't mad when I said that quote."

Teammates such as Rick Cerone may not have liked Jackson but they respected him.

"When it was time to play, Reggie played hard. He had that special trait about him ... he could produce when the pressure was on him," Cerone told the author. "That's a quality that not a lot of people have. You may not like all the stuff that he did and everything that surrounded him, the way he acted away from the game but once he played, he ran every ball hard, he took guys out at second. Reggie was a helluva player and took the pressure off the rest of the guys.

"He wasn't a great outfielder but yet when there was a guy that had to be thrown out late in the game, he was able to do it. Once you got to know him, he was a very decent guy who was just a little bit insecure."

Cerone recalls the conclusion of the American League playoffs in 1981 when it was party time for the Yankees.

"Next thing, you know, there was a fight between Reggie and Graig Nettles at the celebration," Cerone said. "It was at a restaurant and (principal owner) George Steinbrenner was rolling around in the middle of it trying to break it up. It was great," Cerone said, laughing.

"Actually, it was a misunderstanding between Reggie's friends, who he had brought to the party and Nettles' wife and his family over where they were sitting."

Jackson loved to talk and brag and Knowles recounted one example.

"I remember when we were in Oakland and he told us that he was going to go to New York and have a candy bar named after him. He predicted that," Knowles said. "He said he was going to be a big star and he was. He was a tremendous ego guy.

"(Former Oakland manager) Dick Williams once said that when you gave him the red light, meaning cameras and the bright lights were on, he was as good a player as there was. He had the knack of rising to the occasion. He shone when the world was watching. He could carry a ballclub."

Take this from Tony Phillips.

"Reggie always played hard and was always running balls out," Phillips said. "He was always talking a lot of shit. He talked the talk, walked the talk. Reggie always held his head high. He always thought he was that, all that and a bag of chips and a coca-cola and dessert and he was." (that aroused a big laugh from Phillips).

Next in line was former Angels' mate Bruce Kison.

"I was pretty good friends with Reggie during that period," Kison said. "We went out together and did a lot of things together. A lot of things impressed me about him ... his athletic ability, even in his later years, the guy could still run. He had world-class speed at one time. He was a big man, a strong man.

Jackson performed one season in '76 with the Orioles

"It didn't matter how big the fences were. The ball was going to leave. He had that power. I respected his work ethic, the way he played the game. There were times, in his slumps, a manager would ask if he wanted a day's rest? Reggie would answer, 'The way I'm going now, the ball might hit the bat and I'll knock it out of the building and win us a ballgame.' He didn't hide. He would battle. He was out there grinding."

To a man and a teammate, Jackson was a clutch player. Just ask Tim Foli, a mate with the Angels.

"He was definitely one guy who you could put in a glass cage," Foli said. "Put him into the fourth spot in the glass cage and with all the attention, he'd still produce. He had the spotlight on him all the time but he really thrived on it. He worked really hard at his trade, in the outfield, at the plate.

"One day in the midst of a little bit of a slump on an off-day, he wanted to hit. So I threw to him for 45 minutes at Anaheim Stadium. He hit the ball as hard that day as I've ever seen him. It was incredible to watch. He was a unique individual. The biggest compliment I have of him is that he was a team man."

Did he like to mouth off a lot?

> "He was always talking a lot of shit. He talked the talk, walked the talk. He always thought he was that, all of that and a bag of chips, a Coca-Cola and dessert, and he was."
>
> —Tony Phillips on Reggie Jackson.

"It was his self-confidence," Foli said. "There's a difference between just talking and being self-confident."

Having written all that, I'm not ashamed to say Mr. October is my all-time favourite player. He talked the talk but he delivered the bacon, especially with those 18 post-season home runs, including three in one game against the Los Angeles Dodgers in the 1978 World Series.

Just so you know, Jackson is the director of new business developments at California-based Viking Components.

Chapter 10

Clarke hit eight homers in one game

The Texas League is synonymous with minor-league baseball, synonymous with what the game means to small towns in the deep of the heart of the Lone Star State.

The league began in the late 1880s, fought financial problems in its early years and even went out of business for short blocks of time. These days, it's a thriving Double-A loop but its most famous game may have been played on June 15, 1902 in Ennis, which didn't have a team in the league.

Squaring off were the Corsicana Oil City Oilers and Texarkana, which was in dire financial straits and fielded a weak team. Texarkana had become the new home of the Sherman-Denison franchise (which lasted only 11 days) just a few days earlier. The Corsicana-Texarkana game had to be relocated to Ennis because Corsicana's 'blue' ordinances prohibited Sunday baseball.

Okay, so it was Class D ball—the bottom of the scrap bin in pro ball—and apparently the fences were short at the field in Ennis but both sides agreed to play the game anyway. And just think, Canadian-born J.J. (Nig) Clarke, nicknamed so because his native Canadian skin darkened easily under the Texas sun each summer, slugged eight home runs that day to set the all-time, professional record for dingers in one game.

Hitting out of the No. 7 hole where catchers are usually pencilled in, Clarke, 19 at the time, went 8-for-8, drove in 16 runs and collected 32 total bases.

According to reports that filtered out from Ennis later, Clarke realized a windfall from his heroics at the plate. A fan (obviously wealthy) offered $100 to any player who hit a home run and he'd double the amount for any player who hit more than one. The scheme netted Clarke $1,500, which was much more than his entire season's salary.

The fan ended up paying through the roof ($3,400 in total) because in all, Corsicana collected 21 homers, in a 51-3 laugher over Texarkana. Big Mike O'Connor (6-foot-5) was the team's playing manager and that day, he went 7-for-8 with three homers. According to reports from that day, all the homers went over the wall.

It was a nine-inning game and it lasted only two hours and 10 minutes, despite all the offence. Just how bad was this Texarkana team? Pitcher C.B. DeWitt, who was also a part-owner of the club, threw the entire game. The financial troubles of the team may have forced DeWitt to refrain from hiring any relief help. Within a month, Texarkana had folded.

Corsicana went on to post a combined, split-season record of 88-23, their .793 percentage the highest in league history. During one stretch, the Oilers won 27 consecutive games. Their success came about even though pitcher Bob White and infielders Walter Morris and George Markley quit the team in a huff over arguments with O'Connor and team executives. J. Doak Roberts, a Corsicana businessman, was the moneyman behind the team.

Clarke, sometimes referred to as Justin D., is listed in Macmillan's The Baseball Encyclopedia as Jay Justin (where J.J. comes from) and was discovered by major-league scouts while playing at fabled Assumption College, a private Catholic high school founded in 1871 by the Basilian fathers in Windsor, Ontario, located not far from his birthplace in Amhertsburg.

Clarke was one of the last survivors of the White Wyandotte Indians, who settled in Essex County's Walden Township near Amhertsburg. Stockily built at 5-foot-8 and 165 pounds, he batted left but was admired by scouts more for his defensive ability. He was one of the first Canadians to enjoy an extended tenure in the majors.

The power he enjoyed in Corsicana that game never followed him to the majors. In 1,536 at-bats with Cleveland, Detroit and the St. Louis Browns, he managed only six homers, two less than that day in 1902. He also wasn't a defensive stalwart in the majors. He had arm problems and committed 102 lifetime errors in 460 games for a .959 fielding average.

In the bulky, biographical reference book The Ballplayers, one anecdote is related about a game in which Detroit's Germany Schafer took advantage of Clarke's shortcomings. Knowing the sore-armed catcher would have trouble throwing, Schafer stole second, figuring the runner at third would score. But Clarke declined to be suckered into the scheme and didn't throw the ball. Schafer kept up his antics by "stealing" first back and then stealing second again. This time, Clarke fell for the scam and made an errant throw as the winning run scored.

Clarke began his big-league career with the Indians in 1905 in August but a strange twist of events followed. He played in five games with Cleveland before he was traded to Detroit. He played in three games with the Tigers before being shipped back to Cleveland. Yes, strange. Both deals came within a span of 10 days and involved cash. Clarke went on to gain some security with the Indians, playing there through the 1910 season.

Clarke hit .358 with 12 doubles and 21 RBI in 179 at-bats in 1906 and came back with figures of .269 and 33 RBI in 390 AB in 1907.

Shortly following the 1910 season, the Indians traded Clarke to the Browns for Art Griggs. Clarke batted .215 with 18 ribbies in 256 at-bats. From 1911 through the 1918 season, Clarke didn't play in the majors, mostly due to the time he spent in France during World War I with the Devil Dog contingent of the United States Marine Corps.

Clarke returned to the majors with the Philadelphia Athletics in 1919 for a brief stint (26 games) and played in three games in 1920 with Pittsburgh. His big-league career ended at age 37.

Clarke's last connection to the majors was around 1935 when he served as a coach with the Philadelphia Phillies. He was bothered by a heart ailment for a number of years and spent considerable time at Veterans Hospital in Dearborn, Michigan.

For the last 10 years of his life, he was employed at the Ford Motor Company's plant in River Rouge, Mich. He died at age 64 at his River Rouge home June 15, 1949, exactly 47 years to the day he hit those eight home runs.

Boxscore June 15, 1902, Ennis, Texas
Corsicana 51 Texarkana 3

Corsicana	AB	R	H	Texarkana	AB	R	H
Maloney, cf	6	5	3	Deskin, cf	5	1	2
Alexander, 2B	8	5	8	Mulkey, 2B	4	0	1
Ripley, rf	8	6	5	Welter, 3b	4	0	1
Pendleton, lf	8	6	8	Wolfe, c	4	1	1
Markley, 3b	7	7	6	Murphey, lf	4	0	1
O'Connor, 1b	8	7	7	DeWitt, p	3	0	1
Clarke, c	**8**	**8**	**8**	Tackaberry, 1b	4	1	1
Morris, ss	8	6	6	Gillon, rf	4	0	1
Wright, p	4	1	2	Burns, ss	4	0	0

Texarkana   010 000 020-3
Corsicana   629 275 488-51

Stolen bases: Maloney, Alexander, Morris, Clark, Ripley. *Home runs:* Clark (8), O'Connor (3), Alexander (3), Ripley (2), Pendleton (2), Maloney, Markley, Morris. *Triples:* Markley, O'Connor. *Doubles:* Morris, Alexander, Maloney, Pendleton, Deskin, Tackaberry, Welter. *LOB:* Corsicana (12), Texarkana (5). *Errors:* Corsicana (0), Texarkana (5). *Double plays:* Corsicana (4), Texarkana)1). *Walks by:* Wright (1), DeWitt (3). *Strikeouts by:* Wright (2), DeWitt (1). *Hit by pitch by:* DeWitt (3). *Earned Runs:* Corsicana (26), Texarkana (1). *Umpires:* Method and Cavender. *Time:* 2:10.

Note: Boxscores, in those days, didn't list RBI.

Chapter 11

Ripken and Iron Horse two special players

September 20, 1998 was supposed to be just another routine day for Cal Ripken Jr., his 2,633rd consecutive game played.

Instead, 15 minutes before a home game, he dropped a bombshell on Baltimore Orioles manager Ray Miller: "The time is right."

And when Ripken didn't appear in the game at all, it meant that the most amazing streak in sports history had ended. It was a streak (he started all those games) that had encompassed close to 17 seasons and which eclipsed in 1995 a 2,130-game run undertaken by Lou Gehrig in the late 1930s and early 1940s.

Cal Ripken Jr.

As Ripken put it a day later, the decision to pull the plug was "sprung upon everybody."

Ripken simply felt that with a week to go in the season that he wanted to start afresh to ward off another off-season of speculation about his streak.

"There were times in the past when I felt the focus was too much on the streak and that it should have been on the team," the classy Ripken said.

The day after the streak ended, Ripken went to bed "shortly after 6 a.m." and admits he was "wired." When he woke up to report to the SkyDome in Toronto that day, he said he was happy with his decision.

"No regrets, no second thoughts," Ripken told the author and a throng of newshounds in a room not far from the visitors'

Photo by Danny Gallagher

Cameraman zooms in on Cal Ripken explaining his decision to stop streak.

clubhouse. "I felt great about what had happened. I look at it as a great celebration as opposed to a sad event. I wanted to share it with everyone, to actually celebrate rather than mourn it."

But if it was up to him, Ripken would just as soon stay in the lineup every day from here on in.

"When I sat on the bench for the game, I felt a certain strangeness. I felt a little out of the mix," Ripken said. "What the Yankees did before the game was nice. They gave me a salute in a subtle kind of way (by clapping their hands)."

Ripken didn't play that many games in 1999 and realizes his availability will be limited in 2000, an option year the Orioles picked up during the '99 season.

"As you get older, you don't have the same resilience as you had earlier on," Ripken admitted. "This (streak's end) might entice me to work harder in the off-season."

One reporter even ventured to ask if the end of the streak was the beginning of the end to his career.

"That's the wrong way to think," said Ripken, without expressing anger. "You judge on the way you contribute. You say, 'There's that guy who played in all those games.' But in order to play those games, you had to contribute. And if you look at the numbers, I did a pretty good job."

Teammate B.J. Surhoff was asked to try to put Ripken's streak into perspective.

"For him to do that and not get injured is unbelievable," Surhoff said.

That's right. Just think: 2,632 consecutive games played.

It's hard for an athlete or anybody on the outside to fathom. For him to do that and not get injured is unbelievable," Surhoff said.

Gehrig's ironman streak was tied and surpassed by Ripken on Sept. 25, 1995 when the Orioles entertained the California Angels. The breaking of the streak was one of the most momentous of the 20th century.

"I played in the games that Cal tied the streak and broke the streak and that made my career," said Rex Hudler, who was playing for the Angels. " Just think of the significance of that game. We'll be talking about it for years to come. There'll never be a game like it. I'll be telling the story forever.

"I caught a ball in the fifth inning when I was playing second base. I ran it down and kept the ball. In those two games, the colours of the Orioles was stamped on the ball and the umpires weren't throwing many of them out. So the only way you could get one of those balls is if you caught the third out and ran off the field. Earlier in the game, I ran into right field for a fly ball and waved Tim Salmon, the right fielder, off.

"I've got it, I've got it," Hudler said.

But Salmon took charge as outfielders should and waved Hudler off.

"Salmon caught it for the third out. That was his souvenir," Hudler said. "I was cussing him all the way to the dugout. "Hey, man, that was

Cal Ripken ponders reply to question

my ball.' Salmon, said, 'you'll get one.' Cal comes up one inning and I'm saying, 'Please hit it to me. He hit a flare. I caught it and held it up. The fans booed me because they thought I was showing up Cal. It was a dream. As I ran off the field, the other guys were trying to high-five me but I ran all the way to the locker-room so I could put the ball away so that I wouldn't lose it and hope that nobody would take it."

The very moment Ripken shattered the Iron Horse's streak, Hudler and many others at Camden Yards had "goosebumps" as Ripken ran a lap around the field near the fence, doing umpteen high-fives with the fans.

One guy in the back was trying to high-five Ripken so he

went back and high-fived him. "It was awesome," Hudler said.

"After the game, Cal signed a bat for me, "To Rex, we go back a long way in the draft.' I was drafted ahead of him. He gave me two souvenirs in the greatest game I probably ever played."

When you talk to Ripken's teammates such as Chris Hoiles, you're left with comments that leave you with shivers up your spine.

"Everything was very special about that night," Hoiles said. "It was kind of like I was standing there in awe. It's so hard to fathom, what that means, how hard it is to do. He took that lap and I guess it was hard to put in perspective, the greatness of the feat. It's one of those events that was so great and so meaningful. it's hard to put into words.

"I think the greatest thing was when he took the lap. That meant a lot to him, it meant a lot to the fans in Baltimore, the people who were there. It gave them the opportunity to share in an event of that magnitude. It was like he was giving something back to them that night. That's what stood out the most."

Hoiles couldn't help but think that the game and the moment was the biggest of his career.

"I would have to say so," Hoiles said. "I was there when Eddie Murray hit his 500th home run. Both were very, very big events but Cal's was more personal to me. I was lot more close to him than Eddie. Bottom line, he keeps himself in shape. I've worked out with him in the winter. His regiment in the winter is very gruelling at times. He's constantly at work or play, whatever you want to call it. Some people might call it work. He calls it play."

Ripken's streak had surpassed the magnificent run of games compiled by Lou Gehrig, the Iron Horse, who commenced it at the expense of Wally Pipp on June 1, 1925. Pinch-hitting for Pee Wee Wanninger, Larrupin' Lou singled but manager Miller Huggins had no intentions of using Gehrig at first because Pipp had held that post since 1915 and had driven in 113 runs in 1914.

On June 2, Pipp complained of a headache after being beaned during batting practice by pitcher Charlie Caldwell. When Huggins heard about Pipp complaining, he decided to insert Gehrig. Pipp never played first again for the Yankees.

Gehrig played in 885 consecutive games at first before moving to left field for a game on Sept. 28, 1930 when Harry Rice took over first and Babe Ruth pitched.

By 1933, Gehrig had passed Everett Scott's major-league record of 1,307 games. Ironically, Scott's streak ended when he was replaced by Wanninger, the same chap Gehrig replaced to start his run.

There was nothing stopping Gehrig from taking the field every game although it appeared he was slipping during the 1938 season when his production fell to 29 homers and 114 RBI.

Then during spring training in 1939, teammates and the like could see something wrong with Gehrig.

"I remember during an exhibition game in Clearwater, Fla.,

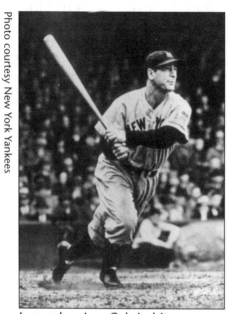

Photo courtesy New York Yankees

Legendary Lou Gehrig hits a home run.

he was going from first to third on a hit off the right-centre field wall and when he was going from second to third, it looked like he was going up a real steep hill," a former teammate, Tommy Henrich, told the author. "He was hardly moving.

"I guess it was over the winter of 1938-39 that something went wrong with Lou. When we got to spring training, we noticed. Absolutely. It was so obvious. If there was a pitch inside, he would have a heckuva time getting away from the ball."

Despite his obvious problems during the spring, Gehrig decided to keep his streak alive but it wasn't long before he shut it down. It became more and more obvious that his fielding had slipped. He chose to stay very close to first base because the lefty thrower couldn't get to his right anymore. Only exceptional play by Joe Gordon at second saved Gehrig's bacon and spared him humiliation and embarrassment. Gordon would overshift toward first base to cover the hole between him and Gehrig.

At the plate, Gehrig could barely muster the strength to get the ball out of the infield on pitches that he normally would drive near the fence or over it. In his first eight games, Gehrig went 4-for-28, all singles.

On May 2, 1939, Gehrig stunned the baseball world when he decided to sit out a game and thus end his fabulous run.

"We were in Detroit," Henrich told me a few years ago. "Lou brought the official lineup card to home plate and then they announced from above in the press box that he was taking himself out of the lineup.

"After the announcement, Gehrig came back to the dugout and sat in the middle of the bench and starting bawling and crying. (Pitcher) Lefty Gomez and I were sitting on the front steps of the dugout and Lefty walks by Gehrig and said, 'Lou, now you know how we feel when we get knocked out of the box (to the showers, usually early in a game).' And Lou started laughing."

About 10 days later, he went to the Mayo Clinic in Minnesota to find out what was wrong with him. He was told it was a case of mild paralysis. Later, the real truth emerged: he had AMS, a chronic ailment that hardens the spinal cord and renders a person virtually useless.

For the remainder of the '39 season, Gehrig remained with the Yankees and made all the road trips, sitting on the bench as team captain. And the Yankees continued to pay him his $35,000 annual salary, despite the news from the Mayo Clinic.

A little more than a month after ending his streak, Gehrig was honoured at Yankee Stadium where the Yankees paraded out their famous 1927 dream team. That's when he made his now famous, stirring speech which included the following words: "I've had a tough break but I consider myself the luckiest fellow on earth, with much to live for."

For the next two years, Gehrig didn't get any better. So when they thought the end was coming near, Henrich and a few others went to see Gehrig at his home in the Bronx.

"He couldn't get out of bed. He was that far gone," Henrich recalled of the visit. "He was a monster guy (once 200 pounds) down to 120.

"When we left the house, Gehrig said, 'Thanks for coming out guys. Don't worry. The doctor said that when I hit rock bottom, then I'll come back.' We didn't quite know what he meant by that but that's what he said."

The Iron Horse never came back. He died at 10:10 p.m. on June 2, 1941, 17 days short of his 39th birthday, when the Yankees were playing in Cleveland.

Gehrig finished his career with 493 homers, 1,888 runs and 1,990 RBI. Just an awesome career. His 23 grand slams remain a major-league record. His 184 RBI in 1931 also remain an American League record as we start another century.

Chapter 12

The all-time, stolen-base champion

Rickey Henderson can talk the talk and run the talk.
Yeah, can he run and he doesn't know when he'll pack it in.

"Shoot, I don't know when my career is going to be over. I have three, four more years left," he told the author recently. "Depends on how many years there are. I try to motivate myself as someone who is a legend and a hall of famer.

"It's the opportunity to challenge other legends, to continue to have the love of the game and joy of the game and when your career is finished, that will be your milestone. I'm not really looking for goals. I'm going out there to love the game and have fun. That motivates me most."

The reason Henderson is still playing is because he stays in tremendous shape. He boasts a body by Fisher, a body to cry for, a body you dream of, a body women would crave and love to touch. Wash-board stomach, that's not bad for a guy over 40.

"The biggest thing is I worked at it. Most people think, 'Oh, you're made with a body and this and that,' " Henderson told me. "But I work at it mostly in the winter time. I make sure my body is toned. I was a football player so I had the football-player mentality and ethic and how to train your body to take the pounding.

"I might be a couple pounds overweight. There are late hours and there is wear and tear and not eating properly," said Henderson, who had ordered out for McDonald's food and was eating it during the course of this interview, but what the heck, athletes are human, too, because they tire of eating excellent food all the time. "Modern-day technology is made to strengthen the player and help hit the ball farther. But I really got into

Rickey Henderson after stealing base no. 939.

Rickey Henderson, now with the New York Mets, is a master at stealing bases.

weights. I do a lot more push-ups, sit-ups and flex a lot more."

Henderson has broken many records but the one he would like to shatter before he hangs up the cleats is the all-time runs record held by Tyrus Raymond Cobb, who accumulated 2,245.

"Runs, that's my job, to score runs as the leadoff guy," Henderson said. "Get on base, get home ... that's quite obvious, that's a goal to shoot at ... it keeps your motivated. You get on the basepaths and get across the plate. If I stick around long enough and the Good Lord blesses me, if I continue playing as long as Ty Cobb played, I should pass his record. If I can compete and the challenge is there, you don't want to just quit, if you don't love the game anymore."

Henderson has accomplished one high-end goal of winning a World Series and he owns the stolen-base record after surpassing Lou Brock's all-time mark of 938. When he reached 939, slick Rick promptly said in a ceremony accompanied by Brock, "I am the greatest." Immediately, he was panned for going a little too far with the statement.

"When I broke Brock's record, that's what made me popular," Henderson said. "People ask me if I'd make that comment ("the greatest") today. I would. Why should I be criticized for something like that. Lou Brock was there."

No. 939 is just one of many record-breaking bags he's actually taken out of the ground and taken home. "Oh man, my mama's got 'em all, all from the ones I broke the records in the minor leagues to breaking Ty Cobb's record in '87 with 97 stolen bases. I have every record-breaking base."

Henderson also has a metal chain he wears around his neck with the numeral 130 attached to it. That figure of 130 remains the all-time record for most bags stolen in one season. Henderson turned the trick in 1982 while he was with Oakland in his first of four stints playing out of the Bay area. The previous record of 118 belonged to Brock, who shattered Cobb's mark of 96.

"I've worn the 130 chain every day since I set the record," Henderson said. "A jewellery guy in California gave it to me. He made it for me. It's my pride and joy."

Henderson grew up idolizing Reggie Jackson, football great O.J. Simpson and boxing's Muhammad Ali. He's met Simpson several times and it was a thrill because Henderson was a football player in his earlier days.

"Rickey was one guy who took a ball game over," said Ron Washington, one of Oakland's coaches in recent years. "He put more pressure on the defence than any player I knew. In baseball, when you're talking offence, you tried to put pressure on the defence and that's what he did easily. And he's still doing that now."

No doubt, Cooperstown beckons No. 24. He should get voted in, the very first year he's eligible.

"I know I have a good chance," he said. "I've played long enough and hard enough."

No argument there.

Chapter 13

He was the "greatest living ball player"

He was one of baseball's most enduring and least understood personalities. The lamanation surrounding him exuded the image of an aloof but fearless ball player who broke salary barriers.

He romanced and married Marilyn Monroe. Yet, he remained private. He commanded respect for demanding that privacy until the day he died of lung cancer on March 8, 1999, thus ending the reign of the person described as the "greatest living ball-player." He insisted he be introduced that way because he was voted the honour when baseball turned 100-years-old in 1969.

Like Babe Ruth and Lou Gehrig of the New York Yankees, Joe DiMaggio will remain a legend in death as he was in life. His first screen appearance came early—in the 1951 production Angels in the Outfield, which was re-created by the folks at Disney in the 1990s.

The evidence of the love he kindled among the fans had its many examples. Think about this one: on July 25, 1948, young kids from a crowd of 42,267 ran onto the field four different times during a game at Yankee Stadium to mob DiMaggio and seek his autograph. That's right, four times!

This on a day when the Yankee Clipper went 6-for-7 in a doubleheader sweep of the Chicago White Sox. The second, fourth, fifth and seventh innings of the game were interrupted when half a dozen fans swarmed DiMaggio, who hit two homers, a double and three singles.

It was in 1941 that DiMaggio fashioned one of the most incredulous streaks in baseball history when he hit safely in 56 consecutive games. A few years earlier, he had gone on a 61-game bender with Triple-A San Francisco.

1B

Note 1B notched on the side of this photo of Joe DiMaggio, who played first base several times with the Yankees in 1950-51.

92

During his run with the Yankees, they won 10 American League titles and an amazing nine World Series. This wonderful player struck out only 169 times during his career. Got that? Heck, many players strike out that many times during one season. Invariably, he always put the ball in play. He was also the first six-figure player in the game when he signed for a hundred grand in 1949.

DiMaggio finished his big-league career with 361 homers and drove in 1,300.

His fabled life became even more fabled after he retired in 1953. We've mentioned the bit part in the '51 movie. Then Ernest Hemingway mentioned him in his classic The Old Man and the Sea in the mould of the Cuban fisherman character, Santiago.

"I think I would like to take the great DiMaggio fishing, they say his father was a fisherman. Maybe he was as poor as we are," the great Hemingway wrote.

Simon and Garfunkel pencilled in DiMaggio as a reference point when they wrote Mrs. Robinson in 1967 for the movie The Graduate starring Dustin Hoffman, Anne Bancroft (Mrs. Robinson) and others. "Where have you gone, Joe DiMaggio? A nation turns its lonely eyes to you," have become some of the most well known lyrics in American culture. "Oo-oo-oo."

DiMaggio thought perhaps that Simon was making fun of him when he mentioned the words "where have you gone?" DiMaggio confronted Simon in an Italian restaurant in New York's Central Park South district restaurant and wanted to clear up any impression that people might have thought the ex-star had disappeared from the radar screen. DiMaggio said something to the effect that he had been doing Mr. Coffee commercials for some time.

"I told him I wasn't making fun of him," Simon told Mark Kriegel of the New York Daily News a few months before DiMaggio died. "I told him the song was about heroes, a certain type of hero. I still don't know exactly why I wrote that line ... but all of a sudden, it was there. Within an instant, I knew I'll keep that ... the non sequitur, the jump. It made the song feel like it was about a larger subject."

DiMaggio's image may have been magnified the most and continued to be a larger subject when he married Monroe in January, 1954. The marriage lasted nine months. When she was murdered or committed suicide in 1962, DiMaggio made funeral arrangements and for years afterward, he visited her grave every day. When he got bothered too much by other visitors to the grave, he stopped going.

The cable-television show Mean Streak that was produced in Toronto in 1998 boasted a fictious scene where a black player hit in 57 consecutive games as a member of the Dallas Rebels.

An actor along the way says this in the script, "What's this, a nunglebun breaking the record?"

Not in the script is a comment from the same actor, "Where have you gone, Joe DiMaggio?"

DiMaggio became a millionaire in his retirement years, simply by signing his name at autograph sessions. One breath-taking, poster-sized oil painting of DiMaggio standing at home plate with a catcher and umpire beside him is priced at $10,000 (Canadian) in a memorabilia store in Toronto's Yorkville district.

Score photo of DiMaggio who enjoyed 61-game streak

DiMaggio made it difficult when it came to getting his signature. Former Yankees catcher Matt Nokes (1990s) approached DiMaggio in the clubhouse for an autograph one day and DiMaggio replied, "call my agent." Ouch. Nokes walked away in astonishment, his face blushing to high tones of red.

It was in Toronto where a certain Joe DiMaggio Jr. took advantage of his namesake by putting his name on a New Mediterrean restaurant in a fancy section of the city near the Yonge and St. Clair intersections. It was tackily called Joe DiMaggio's Wet Paint Cafe. DiMaggio Jr. was one of the owners, was the chief cook and claimed to be a second cousin of the great DiMaggio. The so-called cousin's claims about his relationship with the player and his other insinuations weren't contested by his fellow owners until after he sold his interests in the business and returned to Florida. There was some suggestion that the guy wasn't really a DiMaggio.

I even fell for DiMaggio Jr. when I wrote a story about his supposed connection to the great batter. I quoted the restaurant guy as saying about the ball player, "Joe tells me I'm better at the cooking plate and he's better at home plate. The name has helped me a lot and I have a great time with it but I don't want a trade-off on it. I don't want to go overboard. Joe sits on a mountaintop higher than anyone. He's a proud, incredible, very humble human being in his own right. He was a hero when he played. There are no more heroes like him. The game is all about money now."

DiMaggio Jr., the supposed culinary genius, claimed to have designed 160 eateries throughout the world and called himself a "certified master chef", whose speciality was a soup called pasta fagioli. It was all baloney.

The cooking genius also said proceeds from the sale of painted tables bearing the likeness of Mona Lisa and others would go to the Joe DiMaggio's Children's Hospital in Hollywood, Fla., where the great player resided.

After the so-called second cousin departed Toronto, his fellow owners found out he was bogus and no proceeds were ever donated to the hospital and his claims about designing restaurants were false. The fellow owners were also certain that DiMaggio Jr. was dipping into the till when he was in Toronto. The place did a booming business (Toronto Blue Jays and visiting players to Toronto frequented the place) but the owners wondered why each night's deposit was lower than they assumed. Embarrassed, the owners didn't sue the guy following their background check. And they decided they didn't want a newspaper story done by me because the ensuing publicity would have made them look like complete idiots.

The restaurant later became known as DiMaggio's and as we went to press, there was no eatery at that site.

BASEBALL

(as explained to a foreign visitor.)

You have two sides one out in the field and one in.

Each man that's on the side that's in goes out and when he's out he comes in and the next man goes in until he's out.

When three men are out the side that's out comes in and the side that's been in goes out and tries to get those coming in out.

Sometimes you get men still in and not out.

When both sides have been in and out nine times including the not outs

Thats the end of the game

A humorous explanation of the game by unknown author.

Chapter 14

Breaking the colour barrier

On August 28, 1945 in New York City, Branch Rickey, the white general manager of the Brooklyn Dodgers, held a cloak-and-dagger meeting lasting three hours in a hotel with an African-American by the name of Jackie Robinson.

During that historic meeting, Rickey told Robinson he wanted the superb athlete to be part of a grand experiment whereby he would be the first black player to break the colour barrier in professional baseball.

Rickey felt Robinson would be the type of person who would fit the bill because he figured he had the mettle to

Jackie Robinson as a rookie with the Brooklyn Dodgers.

withstand the humiliation and discrimination he would endure.

"Mr. Rickey, are you saying that you want a black athlete who will fight back?" Robinson asked.

"No, I want a black athlete who will not fight back," Rickey retorted.

"Rickey didn't want Jackie to talk to the press about that meeting. That's why it was so hush-hush at the time," Robinson's widow Rachel told me more than 30 years later. "I wasn't at the meeting. I was at UCLA taking a nursing program."

Two months following the clandestine meeting, Rickey and the Dodgers went public with the shocking announcement that Robinson would break the colour barrier in the uniform of the Montreal Royals, the Dodgers' Triple-A affiliate. Montreal manager Clay Hopper foamed at the mouth about the decision and tried to talk Rickey out of it, saying he didn't want to be the first white manager of an integrated team in organized baseball.

Sadly, Hopper made this now-famous, ugly, racist remark to Rickey before Robinson joined the team: "Do you really think a nigger's a human being?"

Robinson made his silly manager eat his words in speedy fashion—as quick as you could say Jack Robinson. The son of a sharecropper in Cairo, Georgia, Robinson was outstanding during the 1946 season. He won the International league batting title with a .349 average, he was a demon on the basepaths with 113 runs and drove in 66 from the No. 2 hole in the order.

The Royals won the regular-season pennant by 19 games and there was no surprise when Robinson was voted the league's MVP. The Royals also proceeded to win the IL championship before capturing the Little World Series.

Robinson's final moments with the Royals were touching, the stuff of legends. Following the Royals' defeat of Louisville in the Little World Series, the fans at DeLorimier Downs in Montreal stormed on to the field to mob him after he agreed to return from the clubhouse for an encore.

During the celebration that ensued, the mob tugged at his uniform, clapped him and hugged him. They paraded him around the field on their shoulders. Robinson was crying and he finally asked that he be allowed to escape to the clubhouse because he had a flight to catch to the U.S.

When he emerged from the clubhouse again, this time in civilian clothes, he was mobbed again. According to Montreal Gazette reporter Dick Bacon, "the thousands of fans chased him down Ontario St. for several blocks before he was rescued by a passing motorist and driven to his hotel."

That particular event made an emotional impact on a number of American journalists, who were all too familiar with discrimination in the U.S.

"It was probably the only day in history that a black man ran

Robinson was assigned first base in big-league debut in 1947.

from a white mob that had love, instead of lynching, on its mind,"wrote Sam Maltin of the Pittsburgh Courier.

"I didn't actually see that happen because I was trying to make my way out of the stadium," Rachel Robinson told me. "We had many special times in Montreal. It was a harmonious atmosphere. Montreal was a near-perfect launching place for Jackie because of the positive atmosphere. We enjoyed our stay there. I remember people being very supportive because I was carrying my first child that season."

In his very first game as a Royal April 18, Robinson drilled a three-run homer and three singles in Jersey City. Rickey could have easily crossed the river from his office in Brooklyn to see the game but he didn't want to place any undue pressure on his prized project. Besides, the Dodgers were playing their own game at Ebbetts Field. When someone advised Rickey of Robinson's heroics that day, the Dodgers' boss replied, "Is that right? That's a pretty good way to break into organized baseball."

The offensive splurge by Robinson that season went a long way in defusing the racial crisis he had endured all of March and early April during spring training in Florida parks.

Not only that, his dream season had helped erase the sad memories of an incident that took place during the regular season in Baltimore, which was the southernmost city in the IL. After one game, fans surrounded the Royals' clubhouse and apparently stayed there, according to newspaper reports, until 1 in the morning.

In what has been recounted many times since then, the mob shouted, "Come out here Robinson, you son of a bitch. We know you're up there. We're gonna get you."

Accounts of what happened say that three players remained with Robinson during the storming of the clubhouse and they finally left after the mob went home.

Even during games played by the Royals in Louisville during the Junior World Series, Robinson heard the slurs. He was booed every time he stepped on the field or came up to the plate.

The discrimination in Florida, though, gave Robinson the first and strongest inkling of what he should expect down the road.

"Jackie was locked out of one park and ran off the field on another in Florida," said his wife, regaling a story she has told umpteen times over the 50-plus years since the silliness took place.

As late as April 7 during spring training, 11 days before the Triple-A season began, the discrimination was brazenly evident. Robinson had slid across home plate during the first inning of a game in Sanford, Fla. (current home of major-leaguer Tim Raines) and who should be waiting for him but the Sanford police chief, who shooed him off the field.

Robinson was warned by the cop that jail beckoned him if he didn't obey. According to a newspaper report the next day, the police chief told Robinson, "No niggers don't play with no white boys in this town." (the cop should have been charged for using poor English.)

Strangely, just a few years ago, the town of Sanford held a ceremony to apologize for what the police chief said to Robinson.

"Those were really bad times," Rachel Robinson said. "Jackie had to live apart from his teammates, who stayed at a hotel. He stayed with a family because segregation was legislated. Hotels didn't take black people. What happened in Montreal boosted his spirits.

"What Jackie did that year didn't surprise me because I saw him played as a four-letter athlete at UCLA. I knew he had the skills. I knew he had the talent."

When Rachel Isum was introduced to the campus superstar by a mutual friend, Ray Bartlett, she was immediately struck by his presence, although she admitted it wasn't love at first sight.

"What impressed me about him was that he was a very confident young man. He wasn't cocky but confident," Mrs. Robinson said. "We never dated for quite awhile. We would just meet on campus."

After a few months, those campus meetings became official dates and they became engaged.

"We were engaged for five years before we married because I was going to school and Jackie was in the army," she said.

A year following his successful integration into organized baseball, Robinson also became the first major-leaguer to shatter the colour barrier when he suited up for the Dodgers. But he had to wait until near the end of spring training before he was told he would be transferred to the major-league team from the Royals. He was also asked to play a new position—first base—instead of his customary second-base spot.

The 1947 season was eeringly similar to '46 for Robinson because racism still served

Robinson finished with lifetime average of .311.

up its ugly menu. Racial epithets stormed him from all quarters throughout the season. He received hate mail, troubling phone calls and nasty, personal letters from fans, teammates and opposing players, who would spike him on occasion.

The majority of American hotels wouldn't allow him. The Netherlands Plaza Hotel in Cincinnati granted him entry but he was told to eat his meals elsewhere and he couldn't use the swimming pool. Jimmy Cannon, a writer for the New York Daily News, wrote at one point that Robinson was the loneliest man he had seen that season. Robinson was so traumatized that he said at one juncture, "I can't take it anymore."

Robinson persevered and after an opening-month slump, he proceeded to show he belonged in the majors. He hit .297 with 12 homers and 48 ribbies to win baseball's first rookie-of-the-year award which has since been named in his honour.

In 1948, Robinson collected the same number of homers as he did in '47 but his RBI production reached an impressive 85. Then in 1949, he really busted out to win the National League's MVP award by hitting .349 with 16 homers, 38 doubles, 12 triples and 124 RBI.

Robinson finished with a lifetime average of .311, hit 137 homers and drove in 734 runs over 10 seasons.

He was one tough guy to strike out. He fanned no more than 40 times a season. He also batted over .300 six consecutive seasons and was a six-time all-star.

And what a runner he was. Explosive, fast and daring. He perfected the art of stealing home, which is the most daring stolen base there is. He stole home no less than 19 times. With all those statistics, Robinson was elected to the Hall of Fame in 1962.

Over 50 years following the landmark move by Rickey and more than 25 years following his death in 1972, Robinson remains a hero. He was featured on the cover and on the back of three varieties of Wheaties cereal boxes in 1997. It's the first time one athlete has appeared on all three varieties (Wheaties, Honey Frosted Wheaties and Crispy Wheaties 'n' Raisins.

The 1997 season was a special one in major-league baseball because it was played in honour of Robinson. Players and umpires wore Breaking Barriers patches on their uniforms. In addition, his No. 42 has been retired by all clubs, except for those players who were wearing the number prior to that announcement.

Robinson's impact on the game also was the impetus for his selection to the all-century team, a decision that was announced during the 1999 World Series.

Until Robinson came along, only in baseball, did racism reach the level of the outright, institutionalized exclusion of an entire ethnic group. Today, because of him, athletes of all races play alongside each other, as if it had always been that way.

Robinson paved a highway for millions of African-Americans, from athletes to teachers to physicians, to succeed in their chosen professions.

Black or white, we thank him immensely.

Robinson perfected the art of stealing home by doing it 19 times.

Chapter 15

McRae lost title because of racism?

Time heals and Hal McRae, by the sounds of it, got over his bout with sorrow over losing the 1976 batting title a long time ago.

"I've completely forgotten about it. And the events that took place are not important to me at all," McRae told me a few years ago.

Yet, the memory does linger. It lingers because there was a trace of racism involved. McRae is black and he figures Minnesota Twins outfielder Steve Byre, a white man and no-name in the game, supposedly dropped a fly ball by George Brett, a teammate of McRae's with the Kansas City Royals, in Game 162 on Sept. 30, 1976.

"I lost because he intentionally let the ball drop but it's not important to me," McRae said. "I don't ever think of it. It was just something that happened. I don't think George's too happy about it and I don't the guy who let it drop ... he's not too happy about it because I think he was out of ball shortly after that.

"After it happened, I don't know how long it took, but I sort of just forgot about it. And I never gave it a lot of thought. I went home for a day, two days, whatever. We had a couple of days off before the playoffs. And I saw some friends of mine.

"Once I came back, it was time to try and win a playoff game. From that day forward, I never gave it that much thought. It was not something that was important. If I had won the batting title, the incident would be insignificant. I didn't win so it's kind of insignificant. It's not important. I did get a hit. I know the difference was that one hit."

Most of that season, McRae usually hit ahead of Brett in the order but sometimes, they would flip-flop. In the last game of the season, Brett hit behind McRae. There was a battle most of the season for the batting title between the two Royals and Minnesota's Rod Carew.

"Just the last week, we were just trying to win the division for the first time so it was not a battle between the two of us to see who could beat Rod Carew for the batting title," McRae said. "If I had to get a guy over or he had to get a guy over, we weren't battling. We weren't just trying to get base hits. It wasn't selfish baseball. We were just trying to win.

"The last game of the season, it came down to him, myself and Carew. It really boiled down to that one date. That week, we knew we were close enough that there could be a showdown. specifically the last game."

Back on September 1, McRae was hot. The Royals were leaving Fenway Park in Boston following a series and McRae recalls having a "good game" on the Sunday of the series.

"I don't know how many hits I had but I was batting .358," McRae remembered. "I was leading the batting race but I slumped after that. I gave Brett and Carew an opportunity to catch me.

"It was the first year we had won, the most fond memory I had. We really had a lot of fun. It was difficult. We'd been chasing Oakland for two or three years. And this was the first time we were able to win the division. We sort backed in. California beat Oakland and we found out about it early one morning."

I played through an injury late in the season. I played with a pulled muscle in one of my legs, I don't know how many games but I was DHing so I couldn't run. I stayed in the lineup so that sort of hampered my chances. But we were trying to win. The most important thing was to win and not the batting title so I played. I must have played two weeks, maybe three weeks with the injury. I played through it."

After the game was there any discussion with Brett about what happened?

'"No, everybody was apologetic," he said. "What I did was I went home and that was probably the smartest thing I did. I got away. I got time to think about it. I knew what was important when I got back to Kansas City ... you know, to be in a good frame of mind, try and help the ball club win the playoffs. I harbored no hard feelings and ill will when I went back. It was over.

"It was an unfortunate incident but it was over. There was

nothing I could do about it. Nothing was going to change. I wasn't going to sit around and say, "Oh, woe me. Why did it happen to me?' I knew that wasn't going to be part of my program."

Was that your least memorable moment in ball?

"No, the game has been good to me," McRae said. "I have no regrets. I have no ill feelings about anything. You know, through the course of life, in baseball, there have been a lot of incidents but I don't sit around and think about it. I don't feel that someone didn't treat me fairly. In life, hell, there have been things that go on that are similar to the ones in baseball and vice-versa."

George Brett won title.

Deep down, McRae knows that Byre could very likely have dropped the ball because of racism.

1976 AL batting championship			
Player	AB	H	Pct.
George Brett	645	215	.333
Hal McRae	527	175	.332
Rod Carew	605	200	.331

"Well, obviously, it could have," he said. "But that's not important. It happened and I've forgotten about it. But I'm sure that it could have played a major part, a major role, in the decision of the outfielder to let the ball drop. But to say it was, I wouldn't say it was. But there's a real possibility that it was. Even so, it's not important."

Hal McRae placed second.

It's not important because McRae still runs into racism off the field, although he doesn't give direct examples. He no doubt is called names.

"I've experienced a tremendous amount of ill will. I'm sure a lot of people have," McRae said. "Every day, there's a possibility. I've learned not to even react because it's not going to stop. it's a part of life. If I don't react or don't get upset, I'm able to get through the situation or overcome the situation. I can smile or laugh about the incident because I think in many cases, I'm a better person or a bigger person than the person who directs those type of feelings toward you.

"I'm not going to fight back or get upset for what was said or what was done. Sometimes, I've learn to cope with those situations ... just don't react at all. I pretend in a sense that it didn't happen, pretend that you didn't see it, pretend that you didn't hear it. Pretend that you just didn't get it, you know."

McRae, like Reggie Jackson, has been one of my favourite players over the years because he played hard. He didn't cheat the game. He put his heart and soul out there between the line. A blue-collar player, if you ever saw one.

"Well, I've always wanted to win since I was a very small kid, playing in the backyard, in the park, in the streets," he told me. "I would always try to do things to try to win. I hated to lose. I tried to play the game that way."

McRae came over to the Royals from the Cincinnati Reds in a trade and was soon transformed by hitting instructor Charley Lau into more of a spray hitter.

"I was more of a pull hitter and I struggled the first half of my first year in Kansas City. Then I started to work with Charley and hit the ball to the opposite field and from that point, I had good years after good years. But I tried to pull too much when I first went to the American league. And I really didn't understand how to pull. And I didn't understand the importance of hitting that ball to the opposite field and pulling the ball when it was necessary. I was pulling the ball when I was looking for the ball on the other side of the plate. I didn't understand that totally when I first went to the AL."

Charley Lau hitting guru

It was in Kansas City where McRae continued the blue-collar method of playing ball, a very aggressive system of going into second which he had adopted when he was with the Reds.

"Well, we had a passion for taking guys out at second. We had a passion for running the bases," McRae said. "When I came from Cincinnati, I played that way because I'd played with the Big Red Machine. Those guys played that way. When I went over, I played that way.

"In Kansas City, all over time we played that way. We were a line-drive hitting club. It was important that we did the little things that were necessary to win ball games. We had to hustle, break up double plays, go from first to third. We had to score on base hits from second base, score on doubles from first base. All the players realized it. About 1976, the whole team knew the importance of playing that way. Even the big guys like John Mayberry. I was a middle infielder in the minor leagues. I got knocked around and I would knock the other guys around so it was just a part of my game."

Lau, himself, was much of an institution as McRae, Brett and Co. for the way he worked with hitters.

"He would readily talk to you about hitting but he wouldn't shove it down your throat, and if you didn't want any help, he wouldn't insist," McRae said. "He was laid-back but he was very attentive. He knew the mechanics of the swing inside out and was very simplistic in his approach. Plus, he was a person who believed in his guys. If you were willing to work, he never lost faith."

During a game, if McRae or someone else was having a good day, Lau would merely nod his head at them.

"You knew he had his approval and that was enough. He didn't need to high-five you," McRae said. "He didn't need to say anything. I went to see him in Key West before he died (March 18, 1984). He was very ill at the time. George and I went down from Fort Myers during spring training. We flew down with a friend of Charley's, Chuck Ross. He knew who we were but he was in bad shape. We spent about two hours with him. He was out of it. He said some things but he was out of it. He was in tremendous pain. They were giving him a lot of novatin."

108

Chapter 16

Puckett class act all the way

R on Washington talked in quality terms when he was asked what he liked about one of his former teammates.

"The way he went about his business, his attitude, his committment to the game, the effort he gave every night," Washington was saying. "He never cheated baseball, never cheated the game, never did. He gave everything he had every night. He was a very aggressive player, period. He's a quality person, quality player."

The player Washington was referring to was none other than Kirby Puckett.

"It'll be a l-o-n-g, l-o-n-g time before Minnesota will have to retire another number. It'll be a long stretch between Kirby and the next guy. That's only because guys don't stay around as long with the same club," said Washington, who played with Puckett in 1986. "They had a diamond in the rough when they drafted him. I don't think they realized what they had. He turned out to be a diamond."

And if Washington had to redo his baseball-playing career over again, he would've taken a camera with him to the ballpark more often. Just like Puckett, who said the heck with any people who might think he was macho because he liked to have his photo taken with his baseball chums.

"The only thing I remember about him a lot is that he was everybody's dog-damned friend," Washington said. "When he first came to the big leagues, he made a point of getting to know who all the big boys were. I think as I look back, I wish I had that kind of attitude because I played with and against a lot of superstars and I don't have anything to show for it.

Kirby Puckett kept teammates loose in the Minnesota Twins' clubhouse.

"Kirby, he used to get pictures with them, he'd get their autographs. He has a lot to show for it, from the first time he arrived in the big leagues to the end. I never got that. I never tried to do that. I wish I had, to get to know all those guys, to get pictures with them.

"I played for Maury Wills and don't have a picture with him. I met Hank Aaron and Willie Mays. Hank Aaron could come out there now and he'd know me right off the bat who I am and I never got a picture with him. I regret that. Willie Mays, I regret that. Rod Carew was a friend of mine now and I never got a picture with him or Kirby. I was with Kirby for five years. We used to rag him about that. It'd be the team photo or he'd bring his own camera back to the park to get a shot of him hugging somebody. He's got them in his trophy case. All those famous people singing the national anthem, he'd get his picture taken with them."

When Puck's 34 was retired a few years ago following his retirement due to an eye ailment, Washington spoke a few words when he and the Oakland A's were in Minneapolis.

"I told him I always thought he was special," Washington said. "I said baseball is going to miss him, especially the Twins. I told him the young players about the level at which he played and the level at which the game should be played. A lot of people just knew him as a baseball player. Now, they'll get to know him as Kirby Puckett. He's special, he's really special. He never turned anyone down. He never said no. He'd sign autographs all day long. Most of all, he played the definition of baseball. He was the definition of baseball. He was it. He's a hall of famer. If his eye don't get bad, he gets 3,000 hits. He got six gold gloves, two world championships. He could do everything on the field. He could beat you hitting, he could beat you with fielding."

Another teammate, Shane Mack, remembers Puck as a wonderful leader in the clubhouse, a guy who could keep his mates loose, an all-around great player.

"He taught me about playing the outfield and communicating, and as well at the plate," Mack said. "I tried to learn everything as I could from this guy. I was able to talk to him when he first had those eye problems. I just let him know that he had a great career and that maybe God had something else in store for him.

"He really helped me a lot. I was in a situation where I came from San Diego and I didn't get to play much. He really pushed me to get the best out of me. I ended up being a career .300

hitter in the major leagues. It was an honour to play with such a great player.

"He'd laugh a lot. He was a jokester. He'd come in the clubhouse and say: 'Just jump on my back today, fellas. Don't worry. Just jump on today.' He'd go 4-for=5 with a homer. He'd do that."

Puckett, Mack said, wasn't a stuck-up with young players. A lot of times, you get veterans who don't say much to new players or younger guys but Puck went out of his way to meet everyone new and talk to them. When Mack first came to Minnesota in 1990, Puck came right up to him and introduced himself.

"Good to have you on the team," Puckett said.

"We hit it right off," Mack said. "But I noticed he'd go to the other young guys, too. That makes a guy feel pretty good, coming from a guy like Kirby Puckett. He was a great guy, not just a great ballplayer. Good person, good personality."

Despite his eye problems, Puckett has always had a positive attitude and that's why guys like Mack think Puck has been so successful.

"He hasn't been negative at all about the eye problems," Mack said. "Instead of him being negative and saying 'Why me and this and that? ' he's a spokesperson out there for glaucoma and he's trying to save every people's eyesight. He's urging all players to get their eyes checked so it won't happen to them. He's in commercials, magazine ads, urging everyone.

"He's the best guy I ever played with. I played with Tony Gwynn. I learned more from Kirby Puckett. We're very close friends. Tony's left-handed ... it's tough to learn from a left-hander. Kirby could do it all. My thinking about him is that he never really got hurt. He strained his hamstring one time but he kept playing every day. We were so far out of it that they just finally told him to stop playing. He came to play e-v-e-r-y d-a-y. The only time he'd sit out is if the manager made him."

Chili Davis, like Mack and Washington, had nothing but glamorous things to say about No. 34.

"You could go on forever about Kirby Puckett. Probably the most exciting player to watch play baseball and to have played with," Davis said. "To play with him was more exciting than just watching him because you got to see him every day. His love for the game was something that you hope every player that you ever drafted in this game has.

"He had a lot of talent but I just think his desire to play

enhanced his talent that much more. Great team man, best teammate anyone can have. Very giving, very caring, very responsible in the fact that he knew he was THE man on that team, in that organization. He never fought it. He always accepted it. Because of that, his teammates tended to band around him.

"If Kirby Puckett was thrown at intentionally, you bet that somebody on the other team was going down. He was going to be protected. (Pitcher) Jack Morris said: 'If you hit him, I'm drilling your best hitter.'

"I consider him one of my best friends, the type of person you always stay in contact with. When I go to Minnesota, I have to look up Kirby Puckett. Sitting around in the winter time, sometimes, I just scan through my phonebook and come across the P section. There's Puckett. I've got to make that call. He's just a real special invididual. My theory on Puckett is that every once in a while, a spirit, a person is born. and that's their goal in life, their purpose in life is touching other people by what they say, what they do, how they perform and what job they're given. To me, I call it the angelic theory, where when you come up to an angel. You know it ... a very special person, a very special being. I'm not going to say that everything that Kirby Puckett does is absolutely right, correct but 95 percent of what he does affects someone else's life in a good way so he was that right way

Kirby Puckett

with his teammates, with the families, with friends.

"I'm glad he's in baseball in some capacity but I can't think of Kirby Puckett in baseball as someone in the front office. KP can play this game. I think what happened is that he fulfilled his purpose somehow but not totally. He has to do it in some area and that's where he is right now."

Some of Puck's mates may have kidded him about his fire-hydrant size but Davis didn't because he respected him too much. Just think of what Davis said: "You know, you hear about scientists cloning animals and someday, they're going to clone human beings ... if there's ever a candidate to be cloned in this world it's probably Kirby Puckett (Davis started to laugh). There'd be a lot of little Kirby Pucketts around."

For the record, Davis remembers one big play by Puckett and it was in the 1991 World Series won by the Twins.

"Kirby Puckett was Game 6," Davis said. "He made a catch that saved the game. He had a big hit. Lonnie Smith of Atlanta hit a ball where Kirby went up against the wall and saved a run. He hit a game-winning home run. It's funny, you look at him ... you still expect him to get hits every day. One day, he had six hits and I didn't even know it ... I was watching him and I said he had three maybe four hits. 'No, I had six, Dawg.' The amazing thing about him is that he doesn't walk and he never strikes out. He's a great bunter. a very good base runner. He ran hard, played hard. He had a great arm. The only thing he wasn't blessed with I think was the quote, unquote. perfect athletic body. But he was compact and strong. He was strong in every aspect of the game. Where he lacked in the height or build, he made up for in desire, his desire to play. I'd like to know that if there's any one person who doesn't like Kirby Puckett, I'd like to meet that guy."

It was back in 1984 in the early days of his tenure with the Twins when he discovered the shock of his life: a coming-out party when he agreed to partake in an autograph session at a minuscule Minneapolis mall.

"So many people there, man," he told me. "I signed autographs for about three hours, 1,400 of them."

He learned that fans had fallen for him like ice cream does for apple pie or coleslaw does for fish and chips. He had become a quick and long-lasting hero, an unlikely pairing of an African-American in the vanilla-white state of Minnesota.

What he did over time was eclipse the popularity of two other renowned Minnesota athletes, baseball's Harmon Killebrew and footballer Fran Tarkenton.

"It's definitely overwhelmingly, that's for sure," Puckett told me in 1994 about his fan popularity. "Minnesota is known as a white state but it never bothered me."

At one juncture early in his career, overzealous fans would follow his wife home so hubby Kirby solved the nuisance by removing the licence plate PUCK 34 from the car.

On the field, he became a definitive No. 3 hitter and went to the all-star game 10 years in a row. Off the field, he was a genuine class act, a lovable ambassador for the game.

"I'm just a clown, an instigator in my own clubhouse," he told the author. "I enjoy myself and have fun."

Some teammates and rival players chose to make fun of his short, rotund frame by calling him Bowling Ball or Fire Hydrant but he was known mostly as Puck.

"They can call me anything. The bottom line is that they know I can play. I'm the shortest No. 3 hitter in baseball," he said. "I never thought I'd be a No. 3 hitter. I thought I'd be a lead-off hitter or No. 2 or No. 7 my whole career. My mom and dad used to say, "It doesn't matter how tall you are. It's how big your heart is."

That big heart took Puckett many places and should take him to Cooperstown some day.

Chapter 17

Brett intense a player as you could find

George Brett was a guy who played his heart out.

"George and I are best friends, still are to this day," former Kansas City teammate Jamie Quirk was telling me. "He was our franchise, he was personally my buddy, the best man at my wedding in 1983. I have a different feel for him than just the ballplayer. Our two families are close, his brothers are close to me, my brothers are close to him."

Through all the time of getting to know Brett, Quirk saw one trait that Brett always carried into a game.

"He had one style: hard," Quirk said. "He played it so hard that he got himself hurt a lot. He had a lot of knee injuries, hurt

Kansas City Royals photo

George Brett is a legend in K.C.

his shoulders the way he slid to break up double plays. With him and Hal McRae, every shortstop and second baseman in the league feared them both. They would go in there and tumble and roll and eventually they changed the rule because of those two guys. You can't roll anymore, you have to slide. We used to slide and roll and try to take out the fielder. Our whole

George Brett enjoyed his best season in 1979.

team was that way ... we learned it all basically coming up together. George took it to a second level because he was that good."

Quirk recalls Brett as a struggling player when he joined the Royals early in the 1974 season. Around the all-star break that year, hitting coach Charley Lau got together with Brett and in Quirk's words, "What do you want to do? Do you want to work at this to get better or do you want to continue hitting .200?"

Brett finished the season at .282 and went on to post a lifetime average of .305. The pinnacle of his season was in 1979 when he hit .329 with 212 hits, 42 doubles, 20 triples (that's right, 20 three-baggers), 23 homers, 119 runs, 107 RBI. A monster season.

"He had all those triples," I remarked to Quirk. "He had the wheels."

"He could run. People don't realize that," Quirk responded. "He ran better than people thought. He was a really thick-legged, big-calfed guy. You didn't think he could run but he could.

"I remember a streak he had in 1980 when he was going for .400 (he finished at .390)," Quirk said. "He had like six or seven straight games where he had three or more hits. Incredible. He had 27 hits in six games. Just like every day, you knew he was going to have three hits and some days, he had five.

"When we needed a big hit in a big game, you knew he was going to come through for you. He was a great clutch hitter. He's that way today when you get him on the golf course. He never ever comes to play anything to come in second ... card game, golf game, you name it. He's out there to have fun. But to him, fun is winning. Second place isn't fun. He's a competitor."

That's the kind of player long-time teammate Frank White saw in Brett. They started in A-ball together and they came to the majors almost at the same time n 1974.

"I think he's one of the most aggressive players I've ever played with, the best clutch hitter I've ever played with," White said. "He was able to get the big hit at the right time, against right- or left-handed pitchers.

"I liked the transformation he made from the minor leagues to the major leagues. He transformed himself from a good hitter to a great hitter. He's not just known for his hitting ability but also his aggressiveness on the bases and the passion and desire he brought to actually playing the game."

Brett could pull the ball when he wanted to, hit the ball to left field when he wanted to. He could use the whole field. Of course, he could run.

"George was a very good baserunner going from first to third," White said. "He could go from first to second to steal but he seemed to be faster than the other guys when it came to breaking up a double play. His instincts for playing the game were very, very good. He ran the bases, he had the feel for it. He knew the outfielder was going some way and he knew how to take advantage of it."

White couldn't help but mention the batting-title race between Brett and teammate Hal McRae in 1976 when they went right down to the wire.

"The last at-bat for each guy," White said. "George got a hit in his last at-bat to go ahead by a few percentage points and in his last at-bat, Hal hit a line-drive, one-hopper at the shortstop. It just happened to be two guys on the same team tutored by the same hitting instructor. It was just one awesome thing to watch."

Chapter 18

Nine dynamo hitters from different eras

Rogers Hornsby, Ty Cobb, Honus Wagner, Shoeless Joe Jackson, Ted Williams, Pete Rose, Rod Carew, Tony Gwynn, Wade Boggs.

They could hit the ball any place. They were singles' hitters, doubles' hitters, sometimes triples' hitters, as in the case of Cobb.

ROGERS HORNSBY
CHICAGO CUBS – 2ND BASE   1929

Photo from Conlin Collection, American Historical Society

Hornsby was considered the finest right-handed hitter in the game and Cobb was one of its finest from the other side of the plate.

Hornsby's .358 lifetime average was simply prolific. He would stand in the far corner of the batter's box and then he would glide into a pitch with easy aplomb on a perfectly even keel. Pitchers would routinely throw him low and away but that didn't matter to him. He mastered any deficiency anyone might have anticipated.

Hornsby collected over 1,000 extra-base hits and batted .424 in 1924. He was not a tool player, meaning he was a bit of a defensive liability. He had trouble on Texas leaguers or bloopers just beyond second base. He had that problem of balancing when it came to back-tracking on short flies.

Honus Wagner in his olden days and younger days (inset).

Hornsby didn't smoke or drink but he defied authority and was confrontational with management, especially St. Louis Cardinals' executive Sam Breaden. Nevertheless, never once was Hornsby ejected from a game during his career. Somehow, he kept his cool on the field, if not off the field.

Hornsby and Cobb may have been the two most disliked players in the majors in the 1920s because they were aloof and in the case of Cobb, he antagonized the opposition by his spikes-up style of play while sliding into second, third or home. He wouldn't settle for anything but the best. If you saw the movie Cobb in the 1990s, starring Tommy Lee Jones, then you saw first-hand what kind of a player/scoundrel he was.

Cobb held the all-time hits record of 4,191 until Rose dismantled it four decades later in 1985. The Georgia Peach fashioned the art of the triple, which I find the most romantic, glamorous play in baseball because of all that transpires. First, the batter hits the ball far enough into a hole that he might get a three-bagger because of his speed. As he rounds second, the outfielder has usually fired the ball to the cut-off man, either the second baseman or the shortstop ... and then there is usually a bang-bang play at third.

Cobb legged out an incredulous 295 triples, which remain a major-league record. Astounding. He hit only 118 four-baggers but his all-round play and guts made him a towering star. No wonder he earned 222 of 226 votes to head the original pack inducted into the Hall of Fame in 1936. He worked his ass off, plain and simple. He had to be first in everything he did. Sam Crawford, one of Cobb's mates in the Detroit outfield, went years without talking to Cobb because he despied him.

Cobb finished with a career average of .367 over 24 seasons and that record, folks, may never be broken.

Wagner, well, he was a hitter par excellence, a versatile athlete who could play infield or outfield. He captured no less than eight National League batting titles with the Pittsburgh Pirates. He's considered the foremost shortstop ever by some experts in the game and no doubt he's near the top of the list as one of the best-ever.

When Wagner played, he was revered as somewhat of a folk hero and when he quit playing in 1917, the legend grew. Just think: a baseball card of his was purchased by hockey great Wayne Gretzky and disgraced hockey executive Bruce McNall a few years ago for $450,000 (U.S.). Imagine.

Wagner so happened to be one of the original group of five

players who were inducted into the Hall of Fame in 1936.

Shoeless Joe remains a household name because of his moniker, hitting status and because he's linked to the Black Sox scandal that hit the 1919 World Series.

As the story goes, Jackson was deemed to have agreed to "throw" the 1919 series, partly in protest against penny-pinching White Sox owner Charles Comiskey. But Jackson didn't really sit down and take meek swings at the plate during the series. He batted .375.

Because the wheels of justice were slow, Jackson and his Chicago teammates were permitted to play the following season in which he batted a monstrous .382 and drove in 121 runs. It wasn't until Sept. 28, 1920 that Jackson and Co. were indicted.

When it came to crunch time in the court room, a grand jury handed down a not guilty verdict but baseball commissioner Judge Keneesaw Mountain Landis wasn't impressed. First, he wouldn't allow the players to participate in the first few months of the 1921 season while he pondered a verdict of his own. Then on Aug. 3, 1921, Landis threw more egg on the players' faces when he banned them for life. Buck Weaver was one player, who refused to get involved in the fixing of the series. Yet, he was still implicated. He tried to clear his name on several occasions but without success.

To this day, close to 80 years later, Jackson, whose lifetime batting mark was .358, has been left ineligible for admission to Cooperstown, although there has been some movement to lift that ban, partly due to some power-play work in the background by Ted Williams.

And speaking of Williams, he just may have been the finest hitter in baseball history. No wonder he was addressed the Splendid Splinter. He hit for average (.344 lifetime) and swatted 521 homers. And think about this: consider what he would have done had he not served most of five years for his country during various wars as a pilot. Had he played those five years, he quite likely would have threatened Babe Ruth's record of 714 homers.

For close to 60 years, Williams remains the last player to hit .400. He batted .406 in that wonderful summer of 1941 when Joe DiMaggio hit in 56 consecutive games. Red Sox manager Joe Cronin asked Williams if he wanted to sit out the final day of the season to save his average of .400 but Williams said no. He went 6-for-8 in a doubleheader.

The following year, Williams won the Triple Crown with a .358 average, 36 homers and 137 RBI. In 1947, he won his second Triple Crown: .343, 32, 114.

Rose played in an enthusiastic manner, much similar to Cobb, except that he didn't come up high with the spikes. Rose had to squeeze every ounce of sweat out of him to achieve everything he got. He ran everything out, even a comebacker to the mound where he would be out by a mile. No wonder he was called Charlie Hustle.

Rose holds the all-time record for doubles with 746 and his mark of 4,256 hits is still a record he has all to himself.

Carew was a hit machine, if you ever saw one. He wasn't afraid to bunt for hits, to keep a streak going, to keep the opposition honest, to get a close play at first. He never thought it unmanly to bunt. Some players consider it beneath them to bunt or, in many cases, they simply don't know the art of bunting.

Most players are probably inclined to think they would be deemed sissies or wimps if they bunted. They are too macho to think about bunting. Of course, someone like hefty Mo Vaughn probably wouldn't be able to leg out a bunt if he tried.

Carew batted over .300 15 times and captured seven batting titles. He probably should have remained a Minnesota Twin forever but owner Calvin Griffith traded him to the

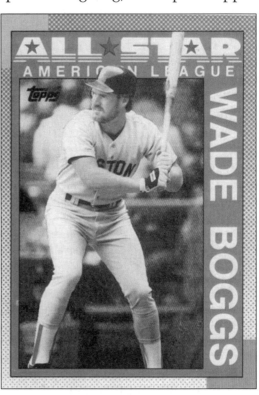

Topps photo of Boggs

Angels because he felt his star was becoming too expensive for his shallow pockets lined with cheapskateness.

Carew played the early portion of his career at second but with his slight physique, he took a pounding and then spent a decade or so at first base. It was in 1977, while patrolling first for the Twins, that Carew flirted with .400 before finally topping out at a splendid .388. Not only that, he cracked out 239 hits and scored 128 runs to win the MVP award in the American League.

Boggs' inside-out swing was one of his specialities, allowing him to go often to the opposite field. Like many great hitters, he didn't have much power but he hit for average, spraying the ball all over the place.

Boggs captured five batting titles, finished second once and third twice, alluding to a principle of not swinging at the first pitch or at balls out of the strike zone.

Gwynn takes a scientific, VCR approach to the game and like Boggs, is a sprayman.

Greg Riddoch, who spent five years in San Diego as a coach and three as a manager during Gwynn's reign with the Padres, said: "I mean, there's a method to his madness. He's an extremely dedicated kid. His work ethic is probably unmatched. His attention to detail ... he will get up in the morning, have breakfast with his little son ..."

And then it's time to plug a tape into the VCR to catch up on that day's opposing pitcher, even if he has been hitting against that pitcher for 10 years. He still wants to check him out.

"And then he'll get to the ballpark around 11 and then he'll look at the information we've compiled on the team," Riddoch said. "He goes up to the cage for about an hour and a half, then he comes down and looks again at the videotape of the pitcher we're facing that night.

"I'd always have three guys in an early-hitting group, mostly my bench guys, but I had to have a fourth slot reserved every day for him. So he'd hit at 3 o'clock and then he'd come back at 5 o'clock for the regular-hitting lineup and then play the game. That's just the way he is. He's such an uncommon person, he's willing to do what most common people won't do. That's what separates him.

"When I was a first-base coach. he would hit a certain pitcher, hit a pitch that I didn't think was hittable. He'd get down there. I'd say, 'how did you hit that pitch?' He said, 'Well, eight years ago, he used to start me out by throwing the ball in here, then he'd go away. And then he'd come back in.' Then in the second half of that season, Tony'd retrack all of his at-bats against that guy."

Chapter 19

Persevering in the face of adversity

There are many good-feel stories in baseball, tales of people who underwent adversity to achieve some fame and fortune.

To follow are just two examples I came up with: Matt Stairs and Lee Stevens. By coincidence, both players turned their careers around after spending time in Japan. Actually, it took several more years for Stairs to start playing regularly in the majors.

Both were bit players at one time, part-time players and then they became full-time players. Both were about 30 when they finally achieved full-time playing status some 10 years after they were signed by their original clubs.

Stairs had bounced around in the Montreal Expos and Boston Red Sox organizations before taking a gamble and signing a minor-league contract with the Oakland A's in the fall of 1995.

Stevens was a a guy who came up to the California Angels with high expectations on the part of management which drafted him in the first round in 1986. He was a left-handed power hitter, who could play first and the outfield. Guys with his power, well, they don't grow on trees. But he was a Kansas City kid playing in southern California and the expectations were too high.

The Angels, especially manager Buck Rodgers, gave up on him because of his tendency to strike out a lot. The team traded him to the Expos in the fall of 1992. On the last day of spring training in 1993, he was cut by the Expos and it was a very sad moment for him and for reporters like me who witnessed the emotional scene at the player's locker in West Palm Beach.

A short distance into the '93 season, Stevens signed a minor-league contract with the Toronto Blue Jays and spent all of that season at Triple-A Syracuse. Then it was several years playing in Japan before he caught on with the Texas Rangers in 1996.

Stevens and Junior Griffey were the first players to hit balls on Utah St. at Camden Yards in Baltimore.

"It takes a pretty good poke to get a ball on Utah St.," said Texas manager Johnny Oates. "He came back from Japan a very good hitter. Some guys go over there and whatever reason, they become more mature. Lee's a good guy in the clubhouse, there is a presence about him. He has the physical stature of a Roger Clemens, Joe Carter and Juan Gonzalez. When he walks to the plate, people know he can hit the ball 350 feet."

For a long while, Stevens wondered if he would get back to the majors. His experience with the Angels helped him grow up. He maintains he didn't know what professionalism was all about in southern California.

"Now, I'm a little more mature," he said. "I'm able to handle adversity on and off the field. I've grown up a lot since I was in California. That's the main thing.

"I put a lot of pressure on myself with the Angels. I was replacing Wally Joyner at first. I was trying to hit like he did to make everybody happy. That took away from my focus and my concentration. I wasn't being myself. I was trying to be someone I wasn't.

"I lost confidence and they took me out of the lineup. I lost concentration. It had a snowball effect."

And then when he was released by the Expos, well, he was devastated.

"That was the first time I'd been released," he said. "The year before, I knew Montreal needed a first baseman. They were a team I was trying to get onto. I got traded to them and I go to camp, figuring I had a pretty good chance of making that team. It was tough.

"As a player, you never think you'll get released. That was really tough getting cut at the last minute. It was really hard. I was in shock all day. I was stunned. I didn't know what to do."

Stevens went to Syracuse but it was a tough year emotionally, trying to deal with his third organization in about six months. Actually, it was four organizations in about 12 months because shortly after the World Series in 1993, the Angels re-signed him, only to release him a month later so he could play for Kintetsu, Japan. During that stint in Syracuse, scouts from

Japan came to see him play. That's where he ended up in 1994-95, $1-million in total for two years with Kintetsu.

"I grew up in those years," Stevens said. "I had to be patient with the language barrier. I was forced into a situation and I learned to calm down a lot."

When the '95 season concluded, Kinestu released all of its U.S. players and Stevens had to look for a job. Funny thing is, for a long time that off-season, he couldn't find a team.

"I called every team," he recalled. "It was frustrating nobody gave me a chance. It was kinda weird."

Finally on March 8, 1996, Cincinnati took a chance but the organization released him March 25. "The season started and I didn't have a job."

Finally, Texas signed him April 4 and dispatched him to Oklahoma City where he drilled 32 homers and drove in 94 runs, winning a late-season call-up assignment.

"It took four years to get to the big leagues and it took four years to get back. That was the toughest part those second four years. I'm a perfect example that someone shouldn't give up."

Right on. The same goes for Stairs.

For years, Stairs lifted his bat way high above his head, a quasi-macho move where his bat was moving all the time. In the end, he couldn't generate the bat speed he so desired. His hands were way up there just the way John Kruk of the Philadelphia Phillies did it back in the 1990s. Stairs' Expos' teammates nicknamed him Kruk Jr. because of his stance and because he also was on the portly side ("That was an honour," he said of the nickname.)

But early in the 1996 season—actually during late spring training involving the minor leagues—when he was demoted to the minors, he made a move for the better. One day as he toiled in the desert heat in Tucson, Ariz., for Oakland's Triple-A affiliate based in Edmonton, he decided it was high time to change.

"I made an adjustment with my hands," Stairs said. "I got down lower where I'm lifting the ball and driving the ball better. I've got my hands down to my chest. I'm seeing the ball longer. It has paid off.

"With the new stance, it's easier to see with two eyes instead of one eye after I opened up my stance. I enjoy going up there with my hands open. It gives me a chance to see the ball longer. The new stance has given me more power.

Oakland's Matt Stairs

"With the old stance, I had too much movement. It was kind of ironic the way I made the change. One day in spring training, I was swinging the bat terrible. It was a hot, hot day and I had a bit of sunstroke.

"I was so weak and felt really tired. It was 110 degrees so I figured I better do something. I was only hitting about ... well, I couldn't even buy french fries at McDonald's ... that's how low my average was."

Being a white guy with blonde hair and very fair skin, too much sun is not good for someone like Stairs. As he played first base after taking some poor swings, he suggested to himself that he should lower the bat and he did next time up. The new move also sees him lift his right leg close to a foot off the ground as he readies to rip the ball.

"I ended up going 4-for-5, 5-for-5, 5-for-5 and 4-for-5," Stairs said of the at-bats that followed his bat change. "At that point, I said, 'hell, I might as well keep my hands down there.' I hit eight homers in Triple-A in 160 at-bats."

Sure enough, those statistics caught the eye of Oakland management and he was promoted pretty darn soon. Stairs was quick to note that each time the Expos promoted him, he was hitting poorly. One time, he was in an 0-for-16 slump at Triple-A, another time, he was 0-for-14 so he figures he wasn't given much of a chance by the Expos.

"My first game back with Oakland I tied a major-league record with six RBI in the same inning. I hit a grand slam and two-run single."

Know what? He didn't play the next day. He finished that season with 10 homers and 23 RBI, including a run of 8-for-17 as a pinch-hitter.

"That year gave me a big boost," Stairs said. "It was nice, an honour to lead all of baseball in pinch-hitting."

By the 1997 season, he had graduated from pinch-hitting duties, although he liked being called Maverick because he came off the bench with the game on the line. Dave Magadan, who played several years with Stairs in Oakland, was called Doc Halliday, again because he was a hired hand off the bench.

In 1997, Stairs' at-bats reached 352 but he showed tremendous power with 27 homers and 73 RBI. It was during that season that Stairs and teammate Mark McGwire had a little contest going to see who would have the highest home-run ratio. During one game, he had a hit in three consecutive innings, a feat that must be some kind of record. This came after he had entered the game in the seventh inning as a pinch-hitter. Incredible, to use a word Jose Canseco dangles often.

"I don't know if that's ever been done before but I know I've never done it," Stairs said.

In 1998 with McGwire playing for St. Louis, there were no more spot starts for Stairs. He was a regular with 26 homers and 106 RBI in 523 AB. On Canada Day, July 1, 1998, the New Brunswick native was rewarded with a hefty contract that would take care of him financially. At age 30, after many years of bouncing around, he was set for life with a two-year deal worth $4.8-million. He also has an option worth $4-million for 2001, plus he received a $300,000 signing bonus.

1999 was another banner season. He hit 38 homers and drove in 102 runs. Mountie is the nickname he gets now. For a guy who is only 5-foot-9, he's a powerful brute.

"The biggest thing is that I know I'm not overmatched. I feel comfortable," Stairs said. "I hit that fastball consistently. Every time I go up there, I try to hit home runs. My approach is to swing as hard as I can to see how far I can hit the ball. If you swing hard and make good contact, good things will happen."

Stairs recalls having to face Cincinnati fireballer Rob Dibble shortly after one of his first promotions to Montreal and Dibble fanned him on four pitches. He was overmatched. Now, he isn't.

There were frustrations along the route to stability for Stairs. When the Red Sox employed him, they once sent him to Double-A, instead of Triple-A. "I can't play Triple-A?" he asked himself and the Bosox.

Stairs was also confused during spring training in '96 when taken off the roster and sent down. He was so down that he was ready to quit. But that day of April 25 in Tucson approached and it changed his career around. On July 4, he was back with Oakland and he's been there since.

"When I got sent down by Oakland to the minor leagues, I was frustrated as hell," Stairs said. "I got to pay some hockey and I didn't want to play baseball anymore. But all of a sudden, I started raking (hitting) again. I was happy I started hitting again and I got back to the big leagues."

Bill MacKenzie, the Canadian director of scouting for the Colorado Rockies, signed Stairs when he held a similar post with the Expos. It was January 17, 1989 in Marysville, N.B., at the home of the player's mother, Jean.

"Signed him for $15,000," MacKenzie recalled. "I'm proud of him because he worked as hard as he could. He had some bad labels placed on him. Some guys were blessed with more ability than him but he worked hard. His success has come because he earned it.

"When I first saw Matt at a workout I put him through in New Brunswick, he was playing shortstop," MacKenzie said. "Just before I signed him, he was named the all-star centre-fielder at the world championship while playing for Team Canada.

"What I liked back then was his hard-nosed mentality. He was hard-nosed and aggressive. He had the physical strength, the arm and the bat. You could see he was an athlete because he was playing hockey then, too, but because of his size, he wasn't going to go to the NHL."

Now that Stairs has security in the form of a sizeable contract, MacKenzie jokes that he would like something in return for signing him.

"I'm waiting for my new car," MacKenzie said.

Seriously though, MacKenzie said he's surprised at Stairs' power numbers "but he's always been aggressive with the bat. With that kind of velocity he gets going with the bat, he's bound to generate some power."

In the majors with Japan in between

Matt Stairs

Team	Year	AB	Pct.	HR	RBI
Montreal	1992	30	.167	0	5
Montreal	1993	8	.375	0	2
Chunichi	1993	132	.250	6	23
Boston	1995	88	.291	1	17
Oakland	1996	137	.277	10	23
Oakland	1997	352	.298	27	73
Oakland	1998	523	.294	26	106
Oakland	1999	531	.258	38	102

Lee Stevens

Team	Year	AB	Pct.	HR	RBI
California	1990	248	.214	7	32
California	1991	58	.233	0	9
California	1992	312	.221	7	37
Kintetsu	1994	302	.288	20	66
Kintetsu	1995	475	.246	23	70
Texas	1996	78	.231	3	12
Texas	1997	400	.276	20	56
Texas	1998	344	.265	20	59
Texas	1999	517	.282	24	81

Chapter 20

Ryan solid from start to end of his career

May 1, 1991, the old stadium, Arlington, Texas. Toronto is in town.

Rangers shortstop Jeff Huson admits he was "slowly moving his ass" into the clubhouse for pre-game warmups. That happens sometimes during the course of a 162-game schedule.

Pacific card photo of Ryan after 5,000th strikeout

"I got to the ballpark and I was complaining a little bit," Huson was telling me. "At that time, I was playing almost every day. I was a little tired and I came dragging into the clubhouse. I was walking by Nolan Ryan and I kind of made the comment, 'Boy, I'm tired today.' "

Chuckling, Huson continued the story. "And Nolan said, 'You should try to play the game in my body.' And then he goes out and throws a no-hitter."

It was Ryan's seventh and final no-hitter. At age 44. No wonder he was inducted in the Hall of Fame on the first ballot in January, 1999.

"I remember after the second inning of that no-hitter when Steve Buechele and I came off the field," Huson said. "Bue was playing third and I was playing short. We got to the dugout and we kind of looked at each other. And I don't know, I think Bue said it to me or I might have said it to him. We looked at each other and one of us said, 'It's over.' "

Meaning lights out for the Blue Jays. No-hitter coming up, folks.

Jeff Huson had fond memories of his days with Nolan Ryan.

"It was a man against boys," Huson said. "And that's the first time in my career that I had ever seen that where major-league hitters were o-v-e-r-m-a-t-c-h-e-d. The only way they were ever going to get a hit was if they blooped the ball in.

"Actually, I believe it was Manny Lee, who hit a kind of a sinking line drive into right-centre that Gary Pettis ran down. It wasn't a shoe-string catch but it was low. But that was the only ball they really had a chance of getting a hit on. They had a solid lineup. It wasn't Triple-A guys they were sending out. That year, didn't they lose to the Twins in the playoffs? There you go."

The relationship between Huson, a non-star during his big-league career, and Ryan, the superstud superstar, got off on the right foot as soon as Huson arrived on the Rangers' scene following a trade from the Montreal Expos.

"The second day I was there, I stayed behind because the team had travelled and they wanted me to work out and get to know things," Huson explained. "We only had five days left before the end of spring training. And they said, 'By the way, Nolan wants to throw to some hitters today so you have to hit off him.' "

Huson started to chuckle as he told that yarn. Hitting against Nolan Ryan. Oh, boy. That should be a challenge.

"Well, I remember my first at-bat," Huson said. "I tripled off the wall in right-centre. And I was just ecstatic. It was just a bunch of A-ball guys who were in the field and a couple of us guys hitting.

"Nolan was throwing and there was nobody in the stands. But to me, it was the World Series (he continued to laugh). And then the next time up, I walked. Next time up, I doubled. Next time up, I walked. I mean, I'm hitting every inning so I got a lot of at-bats. The last time up, I'm walking up to the plate and Nolan's standing on the mound and in his southern Texas drawl, he goes, 'Boy, how many hits have you got off me today?' And I said: 'None.' "

Huson was laughing again as he wound down the story. Funny thing, Ryan, who didn't mind throwing chin music when he needed to during real games, didn't throw any hard, high ones to scare Huson.

"That last at-bat, Nolan proceeded to break my bat and I bloop another single so after the workout, I had the broken bat still and I had him sign it for me," Huson said.

"Really?" I asked.

"Yeah, it's up in my study at home on the wall in Parker, Colorado. So it was quite an experience for me. It's the first time I ever met him. From that point forward, we hit it off real well. I'm not sure why. It was just one of those things ... I was just blessed to be able to play with him. I played in two of his no-hitters, No. 6 and No. 7. I started shortstop in both of those games. I was the starting shortstop in 1991 for his 300th win.

"Those are great moments for me but the thing to me that was the best moment in my career was the day in 1993 we had the retirement ceremony for him while he was still playing. That was going to be his last year. I was asked by some people if I would give a speech on behalf of the players.

"To me, that means more than anything else ... that maybe he thought we were good enough friends or somebody in the organization thought that much of me that I was able to give the speech after the game. There were 40,000 fans. I told the fans that what you saw in Nolan in his generosity toward the fans, his work ethic, the type of person he is or portrayed was no different than what we saw in the clubhouse.

"It was truly an honour for all of us to play with him. He was no different than what he did to us as teammates. If stretching began at 4:30, he was out there at 4:30. He didn't stroll out there at a quarter to 5 or 5 o'clock. If he pitched, the next day, you could guarantee that he'd already be in the clubhouse at 9 or 10 working out before anyone else got there. His work ethic was amazing. I think that was part of the reason for him being able to play as long as he did."

Ryan, 320-300 with 5,714 strikeouts lifetime, formed part of one of the most celebrated classes ever eligible for induction in the Hall of Fame when voting took place for 1999.

"When Nolan first started in the major leagues, he was extremely wild," recalled umpire Larry Barnett. "He was all over the plate. He always threw hard his whole career but I think he became a pitcher in his latter years. He was a thrower. He threw very, very hard. As an umpire, you probably wouldn't want to draw him the assignment because he threw so hard and he was so wild. In his latter years, he still threw hard but he was a tremendous pitcher. I never had one of his no-hitters. What I remember most about him working the plate is that tremendous grunt that he had. I mean, he would throw and he'd go 'Ugh.'

"Nolan's a decent man, a great competitor. He's a class gentlemen. There's a tremendous amount of gentlemen in the game but Nolan sort of stands at top of all of them. He's a gentleman's gentleman. He's the hardest thrower I've ever seen. Randy Johnson is coming close but Nolan did it for so many years. It's a hard thing to do. Frank Tanana, when he came up, him and Nolan were both with the Angels. I mean, Tanana threw smoke also. Then he hurt his arm. Then he ended up basically as a junk-ball pitcher. Nolan started out his career hard and when he finished his career, he was still throwing hard. That's the only guy I can think of who had a career where he stayed consistently hard the whole time. Usually, they hurt their arms or they wear out. He kept himself in tremendous shape."

Which is something Rangers trainer Danny Wheat dwelled on.

"He had very special ability and genetics and all that fell into place for him," Wheat told me. "He had a work ethic that is unmatched that I've seen come through. He had his weight program that he did something different, riding bike, lifting. Whether he lasted two or three innings or pitched a no-hitter, he didn't change. He knew what he was to do after he pitched and he did it.

"The two no-hitters that he had with us ... you know some guys would celebrate, take it easy, take the night off ... he'd always ride the bike 30, 40 minutes after he pitched. Things were no different."

Wheat then talked about one of Ryan's most wonderful of traits, his dry sense of humour.

"He enjoyed getting on people and he fit in very well even though he was in his 40s and the rest of the guys were in the 20s or whatever," Wheat said. "The other guys looked up to him. Guys would listen. Also, he was joking around with his dry shots and everybody would look at each other and start laughing. He didn't do it often but when he did, it was usually pretty funny."

Pacific card photo of Ryan with Astros

When Ryan came to the Rangers, Wheat and his staff didn't try to tinker with the pitcher's training regimen.

"It was a regimen he'd develop over the years and worked well for him so who were we to try to tell him it wasn't right?" Wheat asked. "He was amazing to be that old and do what he was doing. He was a testament to his training regimen he'd been through all these years."

Former mate Art Howe called Ryan "the greatest competitor pitching-wise that I ever played with.

"The key to his success for me playing behind him was his curveball. I'm talking about possible no-hitters," Howe said. "Every time he started a game and he got his curveball over in the first inning, he flirted with a no-hitter that night. It was, like, unbelievable, written in stone. But if he bounced his curveball the first inning, they might have scored off him. If he was throwing his curveball for strikes, this could be a no-hitter.

"The last year I was with him, he broke the record for no-hitters with his fifth one with the Astros. He had several one-hitters. People say his fastball was great but when he would get his curveball over, it was a long night for the opposition.

"In his first at-bat, he hit a home run. Never hit one after that," Howe said, laughing. "I was on second base that day. He hit a home run to left-centre field in the Astrodome. It was a three-run homer. It was his first at-bat in the Astrodome. I'd just come from the American League and didn't know what kind of a hitter he was. I thought he was quite a hitter, too. But he never got close to the warning track after that.

"His work effort was impeccable. He was religious about his weight-lifting, his legs were so strong. He couldn't run a lick. He couldn't run at all but he had tremendous strength in his legs. His mechanics were so good. He used his legs so well that it took a lot of stress from his arm. He was a great teammate, best I ever

Pacific card photo of Ryan with the Angels

played with. I was privileged to be a teammate of his and being a friend. A quality human being. The thing is with all the success he had, you'd never know it. He was just a good, ole country boy. But you also knew when he was working, what day he was pitching because he was a-l-l business.

"The other four days before his start, he'd be joking all the time but by the fifth day, he was serious. He got regimented. He would actually lift weights the night he pitched. He was very big on stretching."

Kenny Rogers, another former mate of Ryan's, had much the

same things to say, just the way Howe was talking.

"One of the hardest working I've seen," Rogers said. And he was very genuine. He wouldn't come and talk to you but if you wanted to talk to him and ask him something, you could do it."

Ryan could be a nasty bugger, too, not just with his high, hard stuff around the chin but he was strong, if someone wanted to challenge him physically. Robin Ventura of the Chicago White Sox ran to the mound to try and fight Ryan after Ryan brushed him.

"It was surprising. You never expected anyone to challenge Ryan," Rogers said. "And when Ventura did, Nolan had him in a headlock. He was a heckuva competitor. He wanted no quarters and he didn't give any either.

"Every day, he pitched, you thought he'd pitch a no-hitter. He had such fine stuff. If you didn't get him in the first two innings, you might never get a hit off him at all."

The sure heat Ryan threw to the plate scared some people. Former Kansas City star Hal McRae didn't even blink when I asked him who was the toughest pitcher he ever faced.

"Nolan Ryan was always the toughest simply because of his velocity and at times, he had control problems," McRae said. " I was not afraid of the baseball itself but I was afraid of getting hurt when he pitched."

Chapter 21

Smith a character and great closer

Tarena Williams had a secret crush on Lee Arthur Smith during their high school days.

She saw him as a hunk but she didn't do anything about it. Smith didn't try to put the make on Tarena either.

That's because of the age-old problem of black and white in the deep south in Castor, Louisiana. Tarena is white, Smith, the bullpen stopper with the most saves in baseball history, is an African-American. A white girl holding hands with a black man just didn't look right. No, no, no.

"He was very handsome but it (dating him) was a definite no," Tarena Bass (her married name) told the author. "I'm not a racist. I don't believe in that but racism is still there today."

At first, Tarena Bass didn't know where an author was coming from when he called her in Arizona to talk about Smith.

"Lee Smith?" she asked. "Don't know him."

"You're sure you don't know Lee Smith, the baseball pitcher?" I asked.

"Oh, you mean Lee Arthur. I just knew him by Lee Arthur, not Lee Smith," she said apologetically.

Lee Arthur Smith is easily the most famous celebrity to ever live in Castor, a hamlet located 50 miles southeast of the Arkansas border, not that far from Shreveport. Castor is farming and logging country and boasts only a blinking light at a four-way stop at an old railway crossing, one gas station, one bank, one laundromat, a flower shop. About 3,000 folks live in that area.

Bass hasn't seen Smith since their graduation year in 1978 but her memories of him are ones she cherishes. She pulled out a '78 yearbook from Castor high school and pointed out a few

Year	Team	W	L	ERA	G	GS	Saves	IP	SO
1980	Cubs	2	0	2.86	18	0	0	22	17
1981	Cubs	3	6	3.49	40	1	1	67	50
1982	Cubs	2	5	2.69	72	5	17	117	99
1983	Cubs	4	10	1.65	66	0	29	103.1	91
1984	Cubs	9	7	3.65	69	0	33	101	86
1985	Cubs	7	4	3.04	65	0	33	97.2	112
1986	Cubs	9	9	3.09	66	0	31	90.1	93
1987	Cubs	4	10	3.12	62	0	36	83.2	96
1988	Red Sox	4	5	2.80	64	0	29	83.2	96
1989	Red Sox	6	1	3.57	64	0	25	70.2	96
1990	Red Sox	2	1	1.88	11	0	4	14.1	17
	Cardinals	3	4	2.10	53	0	27	68.2	70
1991	Cardinals	6	3	2.34	67	0	47	73	67
1992	Cardinals	4	9	3.12	70	1	43	75	60
1993	Cardinals	2	4	4.50	55	0	43	50	49
	Yankees	0	0	0.00	8	0	3	8	11
1994	Orioles	1	4	3.29	41	0	33	38.1	42
1995	Angels	0	5	3.47	52	0	37	49.1	43
1996	Angels	0	0	2.45	11	0	0	11	6
	Reds	3	4	4.06	43	0	2	44.1	35
1997	Expos	0	1	5.82	25	0	5	21.2	1

Smitty's record in the majors

things on the phone.

"There were 10 blacks and 17 whites in the class that year. He was the class favourite, the wittiest, most athletic," Bass told me. "He sang in the choir. He was a real sweet kid. The whole school was behind him. He was very friendly with a great smile. He's a fond memory of my high school days.

"He never used foul language. He was never out of line. He was like a brother. Tall and lanky. The story went around that he could throw a baseball so fast and so hard that he could make it stick in a tree. The ball wouldn't fall out (sounds like a Paul Bunyan tale)."

Smith lettered in baseball, basketball and track and field at Castor high and was voted Louisiana's outstanding Class B baseball player as a senior. He was also selected all-state basketball player and led his team to the state championship.

"There was no football team there because if there had been, Lee Arthur would have probably would have played on it, too," Bass said.

"I've known Lee since he was 12 years old," said Charles Harper, who operates the general store in Castor. "He was always a good, little kid. Always, always. Just a good, young man. Never in any kind of trouble. He was that kind of kid."

Smith was spic and span clean, obviously. The type of guy Bass would have liked to have taken home to her parents except for that issue of colour.

"In my opinion, Lee's a very caring person, a good citizen," said Myrt Williams, who runs Castor Florists.

Smith's teachers at Castor high school remember Smith with nothing but fond memories.

"He didn't get straight As but he had no failure of failing either," recalled Vernon Hough, a biology teacher. "He was real competitive, very respectful. We called him Jip but I'm not sure why."

School principal Nancy Dufang didn't actually teach Smith back in the days when she taught but she does remember the first time he attempted to pitch for the school team.

"I watched him walk in eight runners in the eighth grade," Dufang said. "I used to be married to the coach who started him off (Ronnie Daniel died of a stroke in 1997 at age 65)."

If Smith hadn't become a major-leaguer, perhaps he would have just loved staying at home working in the bush. He became a millionaire and has made life a little easier for his parents, Bessie and Willie B. His parents have a satellite television and saw most of Lee's major-league games.

"Times were tough when we were younger," Willie B. said. "We had to collect bottles to buy groceries. But now, Lee has taken care of us. We have no problems now.

"Lee's all right with me. He's a country boy. I kept him working all the time. He's something else. Yes, sir, I raised him up in pulpwood, pine and oak. Eight feet long. That boy got the work done."

Lifting all that pulpwood, pine and oak, no wonder Lee Smith is a massive man at 265 pounds packed on a 6-foot-6 frame. From Castor high school, he went on to attend Northwestern State University where he played guard on the basketball team.

Smith was selected by the Chicago Cubs in the second round of the 1975 June draft. He began his pro career in Bradenton, Florida, where he went 3-5 with a 2.32 ERA in 10 games. He was named to the Gulf Coast league all-star team.

"When he was just a young man going to the Cubs' spring training, I remember him saying he'd rather stay at home hauling pulpwood than being at spring training," Harper said.

But Smith stayed in baseball, spending both the 1976-77 seasons in Pompana Beach, Fla. The biggest turn of events in his career came in July of 1979 during his second season of Double-A ball with Midland of the Texas league.

It was a move he didn't like one bit. Midland manager Randy Hundley, a former Cubs' catcher, figured Smith was better off in the bullpen.

"I quit. I was going to go home," Smith recalled. "I didn't know how it would affect my arm, having to throw three, four days in a row. Hundley kicked my butt. I went home for three weeks."

Billy Williams, the former Cubs' great, came down to Louisiana to see Smith and eventually convinced him to return to Double-A.

"We were in San Antonio when I made the move," Hundley told the author. "He was a starting pitcher but we were only getting four or five innings out of him. Too many times for a big guy like that, he was pacing himself and being too fine with his pitches. I didn't think he was going to go far that way.

"One time, I went to the mound and took him out. We had a three-run lead in the bottom of the fifth. Then he gives up a base hit, a walk, he gets an out and the bases are loaded with two out. I said to myself, 'You know what? I'm not going to let him piddle around and let him think he's going to get the win.' So I took him out. I was trying to teach him a lesson.

"The next day, we were talking in the outfield and I told him, "I want you to put this ball on the ground and I want you to see how far you can throw it. He picked it up and threw it in a groove three-quarters deliver instead of over the shoulder. That sidearm made him a very intimidating pitcher. When he threw that ball, I said, "You know what? I'm going to put you in the bullpen.' I had to get Billy Williams to calm him down because I thought he was going to punch my head off at the time."

Hundley admitted he put his neck on the line by taking Smith out of the rotation.

"He was very upset," Hundley said. "The organization was not very excited. I did what I felt was best for him and the ball club. I didn't have the authority to put him in the bullpen but as a former catcher, I was getting tired of him pacing himself. I told him he was better if he went hard, pitch by pitch, instead of pacing himself. I knew he had the calibre to be a good reliever, if not with the Cubs, then with some other team."

Smith's venture in San Antonio saw him throwing heaters to the manager's son, who went on to catch in the majors for the New York Mets and Los Angeles Dodgers.

"Todd was just 10 years old then," Papa Hundley said. "Lee was throwing hard at him. It was pretty intimidating but Todd caught him like there were no problems."

As it turns out, Williams went to Castor to talk to Smith and the big guy, the prodigal son, returned to the fold. The following year, Smith pitched most of the season at Triple-A Wichita and was called up to the big leagues Sept. 1. On Sept. 15, he earned his first win in the majors when the Cubs outlasted the Mets in 15 innings. That winter, Smith went to Puerto Rico and in 1981, he was with the Cubs for good in a non-closer role that saw him throw 67 innings.

"I was mop-up, long man but I wasn't the closer," Smith said.

Bruce Sutter was the closer but by 1982 Mr. Smith was the stopper after Sutter's trade to the St. Louis Cardinals.

Lee Elia, Smith's first manager in the majors, kept him a reliever, maintaining what Hundley had been preaching for several years.

"He was a big, strong man, a powerful pitcher," Elia recalled. "At that point, we were trying to make up a pitching staff. He's a two-pitch pitcher with an overpowering fastball and a slider.

"We decided we would teach him to be a reliever. We didn't really have any disagreements then. When you're young, you

Jesse Orosco

Career appearances prior to 2000

Pitcher	Appearances
Jesse Orosco	1,090
Dennis Eckersley	1,071
Hoyt Wilhelm	1,070
Kent Tekulve	1,050
Lee Smith	1,022
Rich Gossage	991
Gene Garber	922

CUBS
PITCHER LEE SMITH

Topps photo of Smith

try to make your way, do anything to be in the big leagues. He made the transition very well. He was the best closer of that era. Seeing him come out of the bullpen, it was a comforting feeling for me as a manager."

Smith recorded 17 saves in '82 and then blossomed with 29 in 1983. He was on his way as a big-time closer. He threw for the Cubs until 1988 when he joined the Boston Red Sox through free agency. Following his days in Boston, he played with the Cardinals, New York Yankees, Baltimore Orioles, California Angels, Cincinnati Reds and Montreal Expos.

At the end of the 1998 season, Smith had recorded 478 saves and he was to pitch no more. During his last three seasons, he had been low on saves — two in 1995, five in 1996, eight in 1997. The most he recorded in one season were the 47 with the Cards in 1990.

Funny thing, though, when you ask Smith about the highlight of his career, the answer is surprising. It has nothing to do with pitching, my friend. Not his first win, not his first save, not the fact he's the all-time leader in saves.

"Hitting a home run off Phil Niekro in 1982," Smith said, indicating his career highlight.

"Really?" I asked.

"Definitely, that's my biggest thrill more than anything. It was a knuckleball. I hit it to left field, following a home run by Jody Davis. I've kept the ball, too."

It was Smith's first and only home run in the majors, one of three lifetime hits he collected in 54 at-bats for a .047 batting average.

"For him to hit a home run off a Hall of Famer, that would be a feather in his cap," said a former teammate, Gary Matthews.

Smith had a reputation for not being a self-promoter. He didn't point fingers at opposing batters, pump his fist in the air or come flying off the mound following an inning-ending/game-ending strikeout.

"That's not my personality," Smith said. "I'm a simple person, low-key, laid-back."

That might explain, too, why Smith never ran to the mound from the bullpen. He always walked.

"Whether Lee Smith had 40 saves in a season or no saves, his personality was the same," recalled former teammate and rival player Larry Bowa. "I think the thing that makes him so great is that he can go out there one day and blow a save and the next day, it wouldn't bother him. He's got ice water in his veins. He knows not to panic or lose confidence. He respects hitters and he doesn't think he just has to throw his glove out there.

"He looks like he's so laid back but he's as intense as I've seen anybody. When he's on the mound, he gives you that laid-back attitude. He'll say, 'Well, here, I'm going to throw it and if you hit it, fine.' But he's an intense individual. He comes across as low-key but once he gets the ball and walks across the line, there's nobody more intense than he is."

Mark Whiten, a former teammate of Smith's in St. Louis, talked along the same lines as Bowa.

"He was the same person, day in and day out, whether he got a save or didn't," Whiten said. "There were no peaks or valleys with him. Sometimes he knows he's not going to get the job done. That's why I think that's why he kept an even keel all the time."

Bob Tewksbury, who had some 25 games saved by Smith, had nothing but praise for the big guy.

"He never carried anything home with him," Tewksbury said. "He lost a lot of games and he blew a lot of saves. He'd sit in the dugout and sat there as long as it did for him to forget about it or rationalize it. Then he'd come in and be like it never happened. And I respected that because he was a true professional. If things always didn't go his way, he never changed whether he was doing good or bad."

When Bowa played for the Cubs, the games were all held during the day at Wrigley Field and usually Smith was unbeatable when he entered the game.

"They had a shadow that goes out there in the seventh, eighth and ninth innings every game," Bowa was saying. "When the sun started to set in, that's when he'd come in. And I said: 'No chance. Yeah, no chance for the opposition.'

"He learned how to throw a breaking ball and everything else. He adjusted with him getting older. A lot of goys who have power, power, power, they say, 'I'm going to keep doing it my way until I can't pitch anymore.' "

Read what former hitting star Dave Parker has to say.

"We had some great battles. Lee was definitely dominating and really imposing, simply because of his size. Definitely one of the best around," Parker said. "The thing about him ... some pitchers are erratic and don't throw strikes but he was very consistent in throwing strikes.

"I recall a couple of incidents. In a game in Cincinnati against the Cubs, Rick Sutcliffe started for Chicago and Lee came in with the score tied 2-2 with a couple men on. He threw me a slider and I was fortunate to get him there with a home run. We went back to Chicago, a similar situation, game on the line, and he throws a curve ball down and in and I hit it out."

But Smith said Parker is not among the toughest guys he's ever faced.

"Edgar Martinez and Barry Bonds," Smith said.

"He was a good teammate," Tewksbury said. "He saved a lot of games for me. For me, it's extra-special. He saved more games for me than any other pitcher. That means a lot to me. He actually wanted all the boxscores for my games and he's got them all except one or two.

"If he calls it a career, I imagine, I would hope he's a first-time ballot Hall of Famer. I think that's a no-brainer. To have played with him ... when my career is over, I can say how lucky I was to have him in behind me 26 times or something like that.

"As great as Lee was, it wasn't always 1-2-3 for him every inning. One time against the Mets, Darryl Boston was up. He hit a forkball in St. Louis. Crushed it. It went foul by a foot. I said, 'Oh, no.' Lee struck him out on the next pitch. I remember that emotion in a good way even though it was suspenseful.

"There was a day game in Philly. Lee hadn't pitched in a while, four or five days. It was 4-2 or something for us. Two guys were on and Milt Thompson was up with two out. Lee threw a 3-2 backdoor slider. It was a strike but it was called a ball. Then he walked in a run to make it 4-3. The next guy hit a grand slam."

Even though Smith was still playing in the majors in 1997, Tewksbury didn't mind saying that Smith always used to nap during games until the sixth inning.

"Every ball park, even Busch Stadium," Tewksbury said. "He took the nap from the second inning until the sixth. He said to make sure to wake him up so he was ready to pitch in the ninth."

And anybody who knew Smith, Tewksbury included, recalls the reliever speaking his own language.

"He'd call money "duckets"," Tewksbury said, laughing. "I don't know how he spelled it. He said he needed more duckets to feed his 'youngings.' If he wanted a contract extension, he said he wanted a contract stension, not an extension. He called food 'grease'. He called the plane a 'truck.' He'd say to the flight attendant, 'What have you got for grease on this truck?' They looked at him and we'd have to translate, 'What have you got for food on the plane?' "

What a character. What a person.

"He'd always sit in the middle seat of a three-seat section of a plane, usually on the right-hand side," said Tewksbury, who also played briefly with Smith and the Cubs in '87. "Headphones on all the time. Never played cards or jabbered with anyone. Just listened to jazz."

If Elia has a favourite anecdote to tell about Smith, it's this one: "He got on the mound in Montreal and he decided he would throw Andre Dawson a side-armed pitch. Well, Dawson hit it for a two-run double and I told him, 'I don't want to see you throw that pitch again.' I wasn't even vocal with him but from that point, if he accidentally did it, he'd have this big smile on his face."

It just so happened that Smith was with the Expos years later when he decided to pack it in — July 15, 1997, to be exact. Nobody else picked him up until the Royals the following winter but he never pitched in the majors again. He was released late in spring training that year and signed a Triple-A deal with Houston midway through '97 but he never made it to the big show again.

"I quit Montreal because I didn't think it was worthwhile sitting around when I wasn't helping much," he said. "Life is not perfect. I took time off and spent time with my kids. It was awesome. I really enjoyed it. Other than during the strike in 1994 this was the first time I had any time off. There were times when I'd go 12, 14 days without pitching. You can throw all you want on the side in the bullpen but it's not the same. I have no grudges toward the organization. No ill feelings."

Just like there's no ill feelings toward Hundley who made him a reliever.

"Whenever I run in Lee, he says, 'You've paid me a lot of money,' " Hundley said.

And when it came time to retiring and doing something else, Smith was back in Castor. Hauling cordwood, raising Charlois cattle, raising his three kids and playing host to many kids from all over the area who adore him.

"Lee's built a gymnasium in his backyard," said Harper, the man at the hardware store. "It's no mansion. It's a modest, little house. He lets the kids in to play basketball from miles around, not just the neighborhood. He welcomes everybody."

On April 2, 1997, Smith collected his 474th save, saving it for Jeff Juden, who became the 100th different pitcher to have a game saved by Smith. Smith is one of four pitchers to appear in

147

1,000 games. The others are Hoyt Wilhelm, Kent Tekulve, Rich Gossage, Dennis Eckersley and Jesse Orosco.

Matthews, a former mate of Smith's with the Cubs, had a few yarns to tell.

"For whatever reason, he was traded by the Cubs to Boston. The Cubs couldn't get Bob Welch from the Dodgers so they traded Lee to Boston for Calvin Schiraldi and Al Nepper," Matthews said. "Not that Boston was a bad place but the trade to Boston to him was like punishment.

"I remember we were playing the Phillies and Pete Rose hits a line drive off Smith, the ball goes to Larry Bowa and we get a double play. We ended up winning the game and I don't think Lee knew it had hit him.

"One year, he thought the Cubs were taking too much taxes off his cheque so he decided to go to the front office to straighten it out. He was told it would take a week for it to be straightened out. But he told me he wasn't going to pitch until it was fixed up."

When 2003 rolls around, Smith will be eligible for induction into Cooperstown. Let's hope he makes it on the first try.

The line on Lee Smith in the big leagues

- 16 years, 141 days of service
- 3-for-54 as a batter lifetime with one homer, 2 RBI
- Committed four errors in 167 chances for .976 pct.
- major-league record of 478 lifetime saves in 1,022 innings of work
- Enjoyed an amazing, 10-season string of 546 consecutive games without committing an error
- Announced he was leaving the Montreal Expos July 15, 1997 and never played another game in the majors
- Signed Triple-A contracts with Kansas City and Houston in 1998 but didn't make it to the Big Show again
- Eligible for Hall of Fame induction in 2003

Lee Smith
with the Orioles

Chapter 22

Cy Young winningest, losingest pitcher

He was nicknamed Foxy Grandpa. He was the first pitcher to fire a no-hitter in the 20th century, a perfect gem on May 5, 1904.

Nobody will ever break his major-league record for most career wins with 511. Mo wonder the pitching award in both the National and American leagues is named after him.

His 316 losses are an all-time record, too. Go figure.

In the off-season in small-town Ohio, Young would cut wood and engage in other farm work involving heavy chores and the result was a strong beast of a man during the baseball season.

That was Denton True Young, a.k.a. Cy Young. When he was young, a young catcher was warming him up as he engaged in a tryout for the Canton, Ohio minor-league team.

Young was throwing so hard that the catcher judged him too fast, calling him a cyclone. Then the moniker was shortened to Cy and thus began an amazing career for a guy who pitched in both the 19th and 20th centuries.

Young first carved a career in the National League that may well have gotten him into the Hall of Fame. Then he joined the Red Sox in the American League and his input there only clinched his berth in Cooperstown in 1937.

For the first three years of Young's career when he toiled for the Cleveland entry in the National League, he pitched with an advantage because the pitcher's rubber was only 50 feet from home plate, which is roughly the distance these days for a softball pitcher. The baseball game's distance had been increased from 45 feet in 1881 and in 1893, in Young's fourth season, the distance became the present 60 feet, 6 inches.

Nonetheless, Young was an ox for the teams that employed him. In those days, starting pitchers rarely got any relief so it wasn't uncommon for chuckers like Young to throw in excess of 300 and sometimes 400 innings per season. For example, Young fired 400 innings per season four times, topping out at 453 in 1892. He won 30 games or more six times. His earned-run average lifetime was 2.63.

When Denny McLain won 31 games for the Detroit Tigers in 1969 and bagged the Cy Young award as the AL's top hurler, he asked for more information on the legendary Young.

"You've done it once," McLain was told. "Cy Young topped 30 victories five times.

27 up and 27 down as Don Larsen fires perfect no-hitter for the Yankees

* 2-0 score, fifth game of World Series, October 8, 1956 at Yankee Stadium against the Brooklyn Dodgers.

* Larsen threw 97 pitches in the first and only perfect game in WS history.

* Losing pitcher was Sal Naglie.

* Larsen's catcher was Yogi Berra.

* Mickey Mantle hit solo homer, Hank Bauer had an RBI single.

* Larsen pitched from a standing start with no wind-up, teasing and keeping Brooklyn hitters on their toes.

* "All the times I was in the wind-up, I was tipping my pitches," Larsen said in explaining the switch.

* That week, Larsen's estranged wife Vivian petitioned the Supreme Court to allow her to get a piece of his World Series share.

Chapter 23

Youngest playing manager

John McGraw did it for a long time. So did Ty Cobb. Pete Rose and Don Kessinger did it briefly. There were others who were playing managers but none was younger than Lou Boudreau.

The Cleveland Indians shocked the baseball world in November of 1941 when they announced that 24-year-old Boudreau would become playing manager of the team in 1942. A vacancy sign was created on the manager's door when long-tine Indians' skipper Roger Peckinbaugh was promoted to the general manager's chair following the resignation of Cy Slapnicka.

Boudreau felt he was capable of managing because of the experience he gained as captain of the high school basketball teams and the University of Illinois baseball team. On top of that, he had completed 2-1-2 seasons as a shortstop with the Indians and he was a freshman basketball coach at U of I.

"I was captain of the high school basketball team in my sophomore, junior and senior years," Boudreau recalled. "That set a precedent. And I felt I had experience with newspapermen. So I sent a letter to Alvin Bradley, the president of the Indians."

But the decision to hire Boudreau didn't come easily. In fact, after the Indians' 12 directors sat down in a room and interviewed Boudreau for 45 minutes, they voted 11-1 not to hire him. But the kid from Harvey, Ill., had a supporter from the board of directors. He was 85-year-old George Martin, the chairman of the board of the Sherwin-Williams paint company.

"He (Martin) got up and made a speech to the directors right there at the meeting about how Cleveland was a graveyard for managers, saying the team had gone through eight managers in 11 years." Boudreau said. "He talked the 11 nos in 11 yeses. It was quite a day in the history of my life. The directors did say I should hire older coaches and that's what I did."

The Indians were 75-79 in their first season under Cool Lou and improved to 82-71 in 1943. Then after three consecutive losing seasons, the Indians went 80-74 in 1947 and in 1948, they won the American League championship and World Series. The '48 season marked the first time an AL playoff game was required to decide a representative for the World Series. Both the Indians and Boston Red Sox finished at 96-58 following the 154-game schedule.

The Indians beat the Red Sox 8-3 in the showdown game and Boudreau was the star of the show. "I went 4-for-4 with two solo homers and two singles," he said. "When I went up to bat the last time, I got a standing ovation from th fans at Fenway Park and that brought tears to my eyes. I ended up walking that time."

The Indians went on to beat another Boston team, the Braves, 4-2 in the best-of-seven World Series.

"I tried to lead by example," Boudreau said of his days as playing manager. "I worked hard to instill more effort in the players. It was a helluva challenge. It made me better as a player."

Boudreau did lead by example. The best example was during that '48 season. He hit .355 (Ted Williams of the Red Sox batted .357 to win the AL batting title) with 18 homers and 106 RBI to earn MVP honours in the AL. "It was a dream season for any athlete," he said.

Boudreau's career as a playing manager with the Indians came to a halt after the 1950 season during which they posted a 92-62 record. His average, though, had slipped to .262.

"Management said they wanted to take away one of my responsibilities," he said. "They said I had to be either a manager or a shortstop. I didn't agree and they gave me my release."

Boudreau hooked on with the Bosox in 1951, strictly as a player. He played in only four games in 1952, the year he resumed managing and the year he ended his playing career. He managed Boston for three seasons and the Kansas City Athletics for three more, including their first season there after their transfer from Philadelphia.

in 1958, Boudreau went from the dugout to the radio-broadcast booth as a colour commentator with the Chicago Cubs. It was a tenure he held until he retired after the 1987 season. That stint was temporarily broken in 1960 when he was called back to the dugout to replace manager Charlie Grimm after the Cubs got off to a 6-11 start. Grimm merely took Boudreau's place on radio. But Boudreau was back on radio in 1961, a season in which the Cubs went through four managers.

Boudreau was elected to the Hall of Fame in 1970. He finished with a career battng average of .295 and his managing record was 1,162-1,224.

"Winning the '48 World Series and being elected to the Hall of Fame are my biggest memories." he said.

Chapter  24

One of Gillick's few mistakes

The trip to Nassau County Coliseum didn't go so great. Randy Smith was only 12 years old at the time but he fondly remembers that night in the mid-1970s when he and Pat Gillick ventured off to Long Island from the nearby Smith household to see a New York Islanders' hockey game.

Gillick was driving. It was a car belonging to Randy's father, Tal, who was out of town watching the New York Yankees in his role as general manager. Gillick was one of Tal's proteges with the Yankees and had stayed behind to mind the Smith kids. Anyway, Gillick missed an exit ramp on the expressway near the arena. Trouble lay ahead. Gillick made one of the few bad decisions he's made in his lifetime.

"Dad had just gotten a new car," recalled Randy Smith, who is the GM these days for the Detroit Tigers. "Pat missed the exit and was going to cut over the median but the card got stuck on the median. I'll always remember that. Pat was upset."

Years later, Gillick was able to laugh about the incident.

"I drove the car over the divider but we got stuck," he said. "We had to get a tow truck to pull me off there. Luckily, a tow truck came along. Those trucks kind of cruise the expressway."

Because the tow truck came along at the right time, the state troopers didn't notice and he wasn't charged with an offence. It was just one of the few times Gillick messed up in a fine career as an executive.

Gillick's reputation parleyed him for many years into the No. 1 slot among baseball's circle of elite decision-makers, despite a streak when he was labelled Stand Pat, when he went more than 600 days without making a trade as GM of the Toronto Blue Jays.

During his tenure in Toronto, the Blue Jays were viewed as one of the top organizations in the game, thanks to Gillick. A scouting-development program, which included the Dominican Republic, is next to none. If you asked most people back in the early-to-mid 1990s, they would say Gillick was the Godfather of all GMs. Under his guidance and savvy, the Blue Jays put together 11 consecutive seasons of over .500 ball and captured back-to-back World Series championships in 1992-93.

"What really separates Pat from others is that he works very, very hard and he's perceptive," said Tal Smith, who is the president these days with the Houston Astros and is one of Gillick's strongest allies. "That's what really distinguishes him. His judgment of players is obviously very good. Other people have had great players but they haven't accomplished near what Pat has."

Pat Gillick

Ironically, Gillick decided before the Blue Jays won it all in 1992-93 to leave the team following the 1994 season. Three months following the 1991 season when the Jays had failed to win the American League championship series for the third time, Gillick revealed in an interview with Globe and Mail baseball-beat writer Neil A. Campbell (currently the paper's sports editor) that he was leaving three years later.

Just a month or so before spilling the beans to Campbell, Gillick almost left the Jays for one of the saddest of baseball franchises, the Chicago Cubs. He held a clandestine meeting—with the approval of his Toronto bosses—in Chicago with Stanton Cook, the chairman of the board of the Cubs. The meeting lasted three hours and the Cubs' dual post of president and GM was Gillick's for the taking. He would have carte blanche to run the show and would presumably have fired the reigning GM, Larry Himes.

Gillick turned the Cubs' job down but not before I wrote about it in the Ottawa Sun. Gillick had hoped the Cubs' overture would be kept a secret and he grilled me on how I found out.

"Contacts," I told him. To this day, I can't tell anyone who told me. He's no longer involved in the game.

Gillick's company-line reasoning for not accepting the Chicago job was "unfinished business in Toronto" because the World Series was still a dream for him.

"We've come close a couple times and I'd like to get into a

World Series and win one before I retire or move on some place." he told the author at the time. "When we get it done, then I might look some other way for another challenge."

It was in Chicago—Rosemont, Illinois, to be exact, a bedroom community located near O'Hare International Airport—that Gillick pulled off his Trade of Trades. Much hullabaloo had been made of his inactivity on the trade front in the first 13 years (especially in the late 1980s) of the Blue Jays but he claims the Stand Pat moniker didn't faze him. If it did, he sure put it all to rest with a blockbuster trade at the winter meetings in December, 1990.

As the winds howled outside and the temperature hovered below zero, Gillick engineered a sizzling tornado inside. He had warmed up the media by acquiring outfielder Devon White from the California Angels.

Then San Diego Padres general manager Joe McIlvaine stepped up to the podium to say, "The San Diego Padres and Toronto Blue Jays wish to announce a good, old fashioned trade."

What followed sent a wail of o-h-o-hssses echoing throughout the media room. Second baseman Roberto Alomar and outfielder Joe Carter were dispatched to the Jays in exchange for first baseman Fred McGriff and shortstop Tony Fernandez. Holy mackerel. With names like that, neither team bothered with a news release and besides, there was no prior leak to the media that such a trade was coming down the pipe.

"That was my biggest trade," Gillick said. "Joe and I had a conversation that November but we didn't have another one for 30 days. We probably wouldn't have made the trade if Alomar hadn't been included.

"We probably could have done a McGriff-for-Carter trade but we probably wouldn't have done it. That was the deal we talked about in November. In the four-player trade at the time, I felt they got an edge on McGriff and that we got an edge on Alomar. But as it worked out, I'm not too sure that we didn't get an edge both ways."

How convenient it was that the Jays finally won for him two years in a row before he left.

Gillick maintains that the previous inability of the Jays to win the AL crown didn't gnaw on him but he said in 1991 that he felt it was time to move on, just the same. Not even a reported $900,000 annual salary (Canadian funds), including bonuses) was sufficient stimulus to stay on. There had been considerable stress for him over the years and dealing with player agents had resulted in adversial relationships because many decisions involving the game are based on economics. The game had begun to cease being fun for Gillick.

In fact, Gillick almost retired one year earlier in the fall of 1993. That November while spending time in Arlington, Texas, at his mother's birthday party, he encountered chest pains and flew back to Toronto where he entered hospital. Retiring crossed his mind then. I tried to prod him to talk about that experience in Texas and he declined.

Gillick was also not interested in talking about that emotional day in the fall of 1994 when he officially handed the GM duties over to Gord Ash, his assistant for many years. Gillick spent part of the 1995 season as a consultant to the Blue Jays but decided to return to the game full-time with the Baltimore Orioles in the fall of 1995.

Gillick stayed with the Orioles for three seasons, resigned, took a year off and then signed with the Seattle Mariners as GM in the fall of 1999.

Chapter 25

Disco Demolition Night backfires

Mike Veeck's greatest claim to infamy got him more notoriety than he sought. It was a promotional nightmare for Veeck, the director of promotions for the Chicago White Sox, the team owned by his maverick father, Bill.

The Disco Demolition Derby was Mike Veeck's great idea of luring fans to the ballpark and it overwhelmed him. The promotion attracted 100,000 fans; 60,000 got inside; another 40,000 were forced to stay outside.

"Everyone who brought in a disco record got in for 98 cents," Veeck rcalled. "We put all the records in a dumpster and blew them up. It was a great visual. We were playing a twi-night doubleheader against Detroit and we blew up the records in between games. How did I know that 100,000 people would show up? We expected 35,000."

Much to the chagrin of the baseball establishment, many of the fans stormed onto the field and the Sox had to forfeit the game. Can you imagine? Bad news, indeed. It was one of the all-time, most infamous, non-game events in major-league history.

"It wasn't a riot,' Veeck insisted. "I've seen riots ... I've lived through riots ... this was just ... all the kids got on the field , ran around and an hour later, got off."

Yeah, sure. It doesn't matter what Veeck says because he wasn't able to get a job with a major-league team after he departed the White Sox two years later when his father sold out to a group headed by current controlling partner Jerry Reinsdorf.

Mike Veeck bemoans his surname being what it. It seems unimportant to big-league teams that Veeck is a kingpin promoter bcause the name Veeck evokes little but negative flak for some people.

It was a publicity stunt that backfired. July 12, 1979, old Comiskey Park, Chicago.

The Tigers had won the first game and that made the fans further unruly. Some 35 police officers were in riot gear, consisting of blue helmets and batons. The police marched through the outfield and restored order about an hour after the melee erupted. Police estimated that about 7,000 fans had formed the melee. A number of them were taken away in handcuffs.

One hour and 16 minutes after the second game was to start, Dave Phillips, the umpire crew chief, ruled that the pock-marked field was unplayable and called the game. Undecided was whether the White Sox should forfeit the game because they couldn't control the crowd. Phillips also said that the issue of whether the game should be forfeited or postponed and played at a later date would be left in the hands of American League president Lee MacPhail. In attendance at the game was Nestor Chylak, the American league's assistant supervisor of umpires.

Shortly after Phillips' decision, Bill Veeck said he had received permission from MacPhail to reschedule the game as part of a doubleheader to be played on the following Sunday, three days after the melee. Tigers manager Sparky Anderson disagreed.

"There will be no doubleheader Sunday," Anderson told reporters. "The game was scheduled for tonight and only an act of God can cause a postponement. This was not an act of God and the home team is responsible for the condition of the field."

WLVP-FM was actually the instigator of the promotion. Anyone cming to the game would be admitted for only 98 cents as long as they brought a record along. It was around the fifth inning of Game 1 that the crowd began tossing records onto the field.

In between games, WLVP disc jockey Steve Dahl gathered thousands of the disco records and packed them into a large wooden box in centre field. After denouncing the popular dance music, Dahl detonated an explosive charge that sent pieces of the records flying across the field. Not long after that, a handful of bare-chested youths from the centre-field stands climbed down the wall and ran onto the playing field. They were followed by hundreds and then thousands of others. The demonstrators set small bonfires from piles of record pieces, threw firecrackers and engaged in fistfights. Fans in the stands, who had grown weary of the shenanigans, shouted: "Clean the field."

The following day, MacPhail ruled that the White Sox would

forfeit the game because there was inadequate crowd control. As is the case in any forfeited game, the official score was 9-0 for Detroit, meaning they swept the doubleheader. Pat Underwood of the Tigers threw a four-hit shutout in the opener.

"These guys don't realize it takes only one injury to ruin a guy's career," Chicago player Wayne Nordhagen told the media.

Chapter 26

Five decades of work spanning 32 years for retiring ump Barnett

Like many baseball players, Larry Barnett jumped to the majors from Double-A ball.

Except that he wasn't a player. He's an umpire. Must have been a good one if he pole-vaulted past Triple-A.

"I was in the minor leagues for five years — the Class A Midwest league for two years and the Class AA Texas league for three years," Barnett told me. "Then I came to the big leagues. I was 23-years-old. I was one of the youngest umpires ever to come up."

That was in 1969 and now comes the time to pack it in.

"The year 2000 will be my last year," Barnett said.

"Do you have to get out?" I asked him.

"No, I'm just leaving," Barnett said. "I'll be 55-years-old and that's it. I will have umpired in five decades. Not that that means anything. But to me, I'm gone."

Barnett doesn't plan on doing any travelling. He's just going to hang out at home in rural Ohio in a place called Prospect, population 1,100.

"Grew up there. Love that little town," he said. "I'm not going to miss the travel. It's a big thing to get off the road. Talk to any umpire and that's the toughest part of our job. My two daughters ... my wife has raised them and educated them. Now, it's time for me to go home. I'm sure I'll miss it but it's time to get off the road."

"Unlike a player, you're on the road all the time," I piped in.

Barnett with tools of trade.

"We're on the road all the time. We have no home," Barnett replied. "I have no reason to stay. Time to leave. You never say never but I'm pretty sure that it will be 99.999% that I'll be leaving. Made the decision the last two or three years.

"I just want to say thank you and move on. It's been a great career, a great profession. Time to do something else. I don't know what that something else is. I'm going to mow my own grass. I haven't done that for a long time so I enjoy doing that.

"That's the great thing about a career like this is to see people like Nolan Ryan, George Brett, Ken Griffey Jr., Frank Thomas. That's an honour. Thye're our game. The players are the game. We're just the supporting cast, always have been, always will be."

Barnett entered the umpiring ranks at a time in 1964 when a chap by the name of Al Summers operated the only school for umpires in the U.S. He's been very fortunate.

"I saw an ad in The Sporting News," Barnett said. "As a joke, I clipped it out and sent it in. I started receiving literature. Then I spent six weeks at school in early January of '64 in Kissimmee, Fla. I was tops in my class."

There have been bumps and bruises, there have been lots of places where he has been hit. "Now it's what you call arthritis as we get older," he said, smiling.

Without a flinch, Barnett came up with the highlight of his career, something that sent chills up his spine.

"Working Cal Ripken's game when he broke Lou Gehrig's record," he said. "That's history. I had home plate in that game. That's bigger to me than the World Series or all-star games or playoffs because that's history.

"Yeah, I remember we had Poresident Clinton there and vice-president Gore. There were tons of secret-service people, Baltimore police and Maryland state troopers. Cal was going around the field and they came out and said, "Larry, how long are you going to let him do this?' And I said, 'As long as he wants to.'

"I'm sure that when Gehrig set the record that no one would ever break it. I can't see it happening with Ripken. Never. It's not going to happen or be broken in my lifetime. To me, that's a remarkable career, to stay healthy. Can you imagine the amount of days he's played when he was hurt or felt bad, when you and I might not go to work? That's a remarkable record, a pretty good work ethic."

Up until then, the highlight of Barnett's career had come 20 years earlier.

"My first World Series was in 1975 between Boston and Cincinnati. That was probably one of the greatest World Series," Barnett said. "I mean, four of the seven games went extra innings. I was involved with Carlton Fisk and Ed Armbrister in that play at home plate. It was just a collision play at home plate. Armbruster broke for first, Fisk broke for the ball and they made contact. In Boston, they blame me for throwing the tea in the harbour and then forcing school-bussing and losing the '75 World Series.

"In Boston to this day, the kids of the parents that are since deceased still yell at me. They remember me. My name is still mud, I guess, in Boston but it's a great sports town. That was a great series. All those home runs, three days of rain with a north-eastern wind. It was unbelievable. Fisk's home run that just went fair ... he was jumping up and down, trying to pump the ball fair. NBC made a four-hour special out of that series."

Barnett has worked in four World Series, five all-star games and eight playoff series. He has signed balls from Edward T. Robinson, Bishop Tetu, Harry Belafonte and except for Bill Clinton, he has signed balls bearing the signatures of U.S. presidents George Bush, Ronald Reagan, Gerald Ford and Jimmy Carter.

Most negative memory for Barnett was the time Roberto Alomar spit in the face of umpire John Hirshbeck at the SkyDome in the fall of 1995.

"Alomar's a great ball player but when he's finished, he'll be remembered most for what he did that day," Barnett said. "That was the most disgraceful, vile, foul thing.

"What I remember is that I was an umpire's umpire," Barnett said. "It's been a great run — 30 years x 150 games a year ... a lot of arguments, a lot of fun times, a lot of sad times, all in a good career. I work hard at my job. Am I right all the time? No. But I think I put in an honest day's work."

Any one argument he remembers?

"They just all run together. We argued with the best, the Billy Martins, the Earl Weavers," Barnett said.

Barnett's starting salary was $10,000 and his per diem was $30 for laundry, food, hotel expenses and

Photo by Danny Gallagher

Barnett relaxes before game.

clubhouse dues. As the 2000 season approached, he was making over $250,000, including bonuses for being a crew chief, and the per diem had risen to $237. Rookie umpires now get $85,000.

The umpires' contract was up after the 1999 season and Barnett would like to see the officials receive more pension money, while the younger umps will seek more salary. In any event, Barnett won't need any tag days when he retires.

"Richie Phillips (umpires' union lawyer) has brought us a long way," Barnett said. "He's the best thing that ever happened to our profession. He brought us to the dance so I'm going to dance with him to the end. He's like a bull in a china shop. He's our maestro."

This interview was conducted before the umpires' negotiating fiasco in the summer of 1999 but Barnett was not one of the umpires who tendered his resignation. As it stands, he has been retained for the 2000 season, his final in the majors.

Chapter 27

First, there was hickory, then there was ash, and along came maple

He was born in Kansas City, Missouri and grew up in central South Dakota in Wessington Springs, a town of "4,000 souls," as he describes it, some 200 miles south of Aberdeen.

Sam Holman is a carpenter and setmaker/stagehand, who made baseball history when he introduced a bat manufactured of Canadian rock maple for the major leagues officially during the 1998 season, although some Toronto Blue Jays' players were discreetly using the lumber in 1997.

"I don't think we'll ever supplant an ash bat but we can certainly give it a run for its money," Holman told the author. "Finally after 200 years, there's a choice but we have our work cut out for us. You have to remember that ash bats have 200 years under their belts. The people who make them know what they're doing."

It was in K.C. where Holman struck a chord or a connection with trees that would help him carve a place in baseball's record books. Cooperstown has one of his bats in the Hall of Fame. A nice feather in his cap.

"My grandfather was a whittler," Holman said. "He whittled the pine and woods, so I learned how to whittle. Eastern white pine and walnut were the favourite woods to whittle, mainly because Missouri has a lot of walnut and it's a very pretty wood.

Missouri walnut is extremely pretty."

When Holman moved to South Dakota, his love for wood continued as he was introduced specifically to a state full of maple trees. He also spent time around cattle because his father was a veternarian. He lived in South Dakota until he graduated from high school.

Later, he spent several years bouncing around Europe, mostly in England. He tried to learn French in Switzerland and then joined the U.S. army for a stint that included a posting to Germany.

"I guess that's about the most athletic I ever got in my life," Holman said. "I dodged beer steins."

Funny Holman should mention beer steins because a silver, tin beer stein awaits him each time he, resplendent in his trademark silver-striped overalls, enters the Mayflower bar in midtown Ottawa on Elgin St., located not far from the Peace Tower and Parliament Hill.

In 1972, Holman landed in Sarnia, Ont., where he married a girl from that small city but when it came time to further his education, the couple moved to Ottawa and he attended Carleton University where he completed three years of an Eng-

Sam Holman posing with bats he's made.

lish literature course. He soon discovered he wasn't much of an academic so he began working at the National Arts Centre.

"I served the artistic community for 23 years after that," Holman told me. "I was involved in putting up all kinds of live-entertainment shows. Baseball and live entertainment are very much inter-connected. The NAC wasn't really built and they needed young people who were willing to stay up all day and all night putting up sets ... that's how I started.

167

"Opera is a very interesting connection. It's really the first professional experience I had with people who dealt with wood every day. Believe me, we talked about it all the time, whether you're talking with the first violinist in the orchestra or a ballerina. The arts centre had a beautifully sprung floor made of spruce. These people they live on wood. Wood is what makes them excellent. I've always said one of the best discussions on wood was with a baseball player, a violinist and a ballerina ... as good a discussion on wood that would really blow your socks off."

Talk about wood, hickory bats were utilized way back in the 1800s, then it was ash for much of the 20th century. But in 1995, a friend of Holman's, Bill MacKenzie, the Colorado Rockies' director of Canadian scouting, suggested he try his hand at making a new type of bat because too many ash bats were being broken by major-league players.

Logo used by bat maker Sam Holman.

Holman (Creemore) and MacKenzie (Labatt Blue) have quaffed many a pint of beer in that Mayflower bar in Ottawa and sure enough, Holman took MacKenzie up on his suggestion. So what did Holman do? He purchased a $6,000 Italian lathe from Kevin Rintoul of Carleton Place, Ont., who owned a lot on the Mississippi River (the Canadian one).

"It's a good basic machine but it is a 1945 machine," Holman said. "It was basically used to make axe handles."

As Holman explained, it takes 30 minutes to make a bat. The rough spiral can be done in about 2 minutes. It takes 15 minutes to carve a bat, just as long to sand it.

In the early spring of 1996, Holman began making prototype bats in the small basement of his west-Ottawa home and by April of 1997, he submitted some for approval to Bill Murray in the commissioner's office in New York.

Holman waited and waited for the approval to come so his bats could be legitimately used in the big leagues. While he waited, he gave some bats to major-leaguers such as Joe Carter of the Blue Jays, who used the bat on several occasions during the '97 season, discretely, of course. He even hit a home run in Kansas City where Royals' catcher Mike Sweeney commented on the bat's difference.

Finally in February of 1998, Holman got the good news from Murray. He finally was allowed to have players legally use bats in a regular-season game. Long before he gave his approval, Murray remarked, "Is this real wood?"

Holman and his company, The Original Maple Bat Company, boast only a small share of the major-league market but he says "we're competing at a very high level. But we're far from perfect. We have our work cut out for us."

In 1999, Holman made 3,000 bats while Hillerich and Bradsby, the maker of the ultra-famous Louisville Slugger, a long-time ash-bat stalwart, routinely manufactures a million pieces of lumber per annum. How do you compete with that?

It took an initial investment of $20,000 (Canadian) by Holman to start up operations and since then, the bill has climbed to six figures. Holman said it costs $7,000 to purchase 800 pieces of wood necessary for an order to be placed with a firm in Shawinigan, Quebec, which he jokingly refers to as Canadian Prime Minister Jean Chretien's "backyard." That firm specializes in high-end hardwood that is also used in the formation of guitars.

"It's hard to build anything in a day," Holman said. "It's an uphill battle. What people don't understand is that this takes a lot of research and development.

"The professional uses a tee-ball exercise to locate the sweet spot on any wooden bat before batting practice. This simple exercise also saves bats while allowing the player to evaluate his swing. The effective sweet spot on a wooden bat is the size of a pencil eraser and the home run comes off the pencil point."

Holman likes to think there's a sharper, sweeter, crisper sound emanating from a maple bat as compared to an ash one. Maple bats, he says, consist of a more dense, heavier wood than ash, not to mention boasting a higher grain.

Holman informed the Hall of Fame in Cooperstown what he was doing and officials there asked him to send a bat to be placed in its hallowed surroundings. Hey, it's history. Maple bats are tougher to break, even when you're jammed with a pitch and you may only have the handle of the bat in your hand. Ash bats tend to crack easier than maple ones. Holman notes that Sammy Sosa hit a broken-bat homer, using a Sam Bat.

Holman's clients include Barry Bonds, Jose Canseco, Royce Clayton, Stan Javier, Vladimir Guerrero, Carlos Delgado and Craig Biggio, to name a few. Holman charges $60 Canadian or $43 U.S. for one Sam Bat. The Expos initially shied away from the bat but Holman worked hard to gain their trust.

"As soon as Vladimir picked up the bat, the whole Expos' team kind of swung over to it," Holman said. "The Expos see the durability and the cost effectiveness."

During spring training in 1999, Holman travelled to the Cactus League in Arizona to follow up on the sales pitches he had made since his launch of the bat. He met up with Bonds and ended up having a chat of about an hour once San Francisco Giants' teammate Brent Mayne sort of broke the ice by telling Holman, "Well, you have to approach him and find out."

Bonds, at the best of times, can be a real pain in the ass, especially with the media. But Holman went up to Bonds and asked him about the bat. Carter had obviously told Bonds that the Sam Bat was something special so Bonds surprised Holman by saying, "Make all you want."

At that point, Holman said Bonds took one of the Sam Bat models the manufacturer was carrying with him during spring training and proceeded to blast a few balls over the centre-field fence. After finishing his batting session, Bonds waltzed right over to tell Holman, "I've never hit balls over the centre-field fence like that."

Bonds then sat in the dugout with Holman for an hour to talk. Along the way, a clubhouse boy asked Bonds if he would break a lot more records if he was using a Sam Bat and Bonds replied, "it doesn't matter now. I'm in the Hall of Fame."

Slowly but surely, the Sam Bat legend is gaining steam. A Sports Illustrated article in September of 1999 appeared under the headline Sam Takes On Sluggers. Holman and his product have also been featured in the New York Times and many Canadian papers.

Hopefully in the 21st century, his maple bats will thrive to gain a bigger share of the bat market. You can't help but cheer for an underdog.

Abner Doubleday is called by many as the inventor of baseball but it's believed that the game was founded in St. Mary's, Ontario near Toronto in the 1800s.

Index

What the media said about Danny Gallagher's previous books relating to baseball

You Don't Forget Homers Like That:
Memories of Strawberry, Cosby and the Expos

"For fans and fellow lovers of the sport, and the home team in particular, this book is likely to add another dimension to the endless fascination baseball evokes in the true believer."
— Montreal Gazette.

"Un livre de baseball p-a-s-s-i-o-n-a-n-t. Gallagher aime le baseball avec une passion."
— Rejean Tremblay, La Presse, Montreal.

"Gallagher has taken his devotion of the game to a new level. There have been two things Gallagher has loved about baseball — playing it and writing it."
— Peter Clark, The Mercury, Renfrew, Ont.

"A book with juicy details." — CFCF-TV, Montreal.

"Wonderful, new book." — CJAD Radio, Montreal.

"Great entertainment for an Expos' fan."
— CIQC Radio, Montreal.

"Literary home run." — The Leader, Eganville, Ont.

Angels' Halo Haunted:
Baseball Tragedies Revisited

"Here are 20 extended vignettes of baseball misery. The book's focus is on the Angels' long history of tragedy and near tragedy. Perhaps wearing a halo as your emblem is just tempting fate."   — Martin Levin, The Globe and Mail, Toronto.

"A very heart-wrenching, riveting collection of stories on baseball's greatest tragedies."
— WBOB All-Sports Radio, Cincinatti.

"This book is believed to be the first such compilation of baseball tragedies."
— The Leader, Eganville, Ont.

Notes and Autographs